BREAKING
THE
BASTARD
SPIRIT

BREAKING
THE
BASTARD
SPIRIT

WHY THE CHURCH NEEDS FATHERS
NOW MORE THAN EVER!

REN SCHUFFMAN
TERRY CUTHBERTSON

Published by …Freedom Fellowship Church 320 S Symes Ln Mustang OK 73064

Paperback ISBN: 978-1-7368581-0-3
Ebook ISBN: 978-1-7368581-1-0

Printed in the United States of America

Endorsements

As a spiritual mom, and sometimes dad, to thousands of leaders in the world today, the thing I am challenged with the most is making sure that I am constantly aware of where my heart is towards those that look to me as that person. My number one motive, as someone who leads leaders or as someone who instructs leaders or as someone who loves leaders enough to live a life in front of them that exemplifies the character of Jesus Christ, is to show up.

I'll be the first to admit I'm not always that person. When I'm not, I leave devastation and wound the very ones that I'm trying to love. When we wound the next generation through abandoning their ideas or rejecting their gifts/talents etc. more than we position ourselves to show up and listen, we are responsible for creating, what Ren and Terry have creatively called a Bastard Spirit. In other words, we let down the very generation that we are responsible to create. And what that produces is an insecure generation that feels they have to perform for acceptance more than just knowing they belong.

Knowing that there are fathers/mothers who will walk alongside them will greatly help them to believe that they can become everything that Father God created within them as sons and daughters. This book will span the time of longevity and become an instrument in the hands of a generation who will break this spirit in relationships.

Good job Guys; proud of you!

-Trisha Frost, Co-Founder Shiloh Place Ministries

I love this book that Pastor Ren and Pastor Terry have written together! While much has been written recently on the topic of sonship and orphanhood, much less has been written on how to be a spiritual father – which is just as important! I believe this book is a key contribution to raising up not just sons, but fathers, and helping the body of Christ continue to grow up in every way into what the Father has for her to be.

-Putty Putman, School of Kingdom Ministry Founder, Author of Live Like Jesus and Kingdom Impact

Pastor Ren Schuffman and Pastor Terry Cuthbertson have written a very important and much needed word for our time. "Breaking the Bastard Spirit" is one of the most well articulated and detailed expositions concerning our generation. I have spent many years studying and teaching about the importance of overcoming an orphan spirit and a fatherless generation. I am sincerely grateful that Pastor Ren and Pastor Terry have taken the time to write this valuable Word for those who have been struggling for many years. I personally believe that this book will be a tremendous key for the fatherless and for those who are called to be fathers and mothers.

-Ryan Johnson, Author of *How to Contend for Your Miracle*

This book is an incredible illustration of what the true church should look like. I could not stop reading it. This is what we need in our everyday lives, true fathers that can build up the body of Christ and love others the way Jesus does. Ren is the perfect demonstration of his book. I have experienced first-hand his love for others, including myself and my family. He took us under his wings and has been a spiritual father to me, something I had never experienced before. It has caused me to grow in leaps and bounds but, above all, to grow in my relationship with the Father.

This book will change your life and how you see others. The body of Christ truly needs Fathers to guide and love them. This book is truly the Father's heart in words.

-Sharell Barerra - Revivalist, prophetic voice
and Pastor of 509 Revival Hub in WA

Dedication

Ren's Dedication

I dedicate this book to the love of my life, my incredible wife, Rachael, my three amazing sons, Isaiah, Eli, and Caleb, and my amazing church leadership that has allowed me to be a father to them. The fruit of my life is found in you. I hope that this book will truly spell out what I have tried to live out.

Terry's Dedication

This book is dedicated to my amazing gift from God, my family! To Nina, thank you for supporting all my crazy dreams and loving me for me. You are my confidante, my friend, and my love! To my incredible kids, Alyssa, Ayla, and Ashton, You guys are my greatest blessing. I love being your dad!

CONTENTS

THE RISE OF A SPIRITUALLY FATHERLESS GENERATION

As you read this book and the stories about the rise of a spiritually fatherless generation, you might find it peculiar that God chose two men who have never had spiritual fathers. You might find it odd that men that have never walked as spiritual sons would be able to release revelation and wisdom on the need for spiritual fathers. Neither of us have had spiritual fathers in our lives, but it is through God's grace and intervention that we have both become spiritual fathers and raised up healthy and powerful sons and daughters in the kingdom.

Isn't it just like God to use the foolish things of man to confound the wise? Our unique perspective of fighting through and overcoming fatherlessness in both the physical and the spiritual has carved a perfect spot in our hearts to place spiritual children in. We have both successfully raised children in the physical and spiritual. We have seen how the fatherless heart has created bastards – those without a true father to claim them, while we have watched as it has turned the modern church into an orphanage. The orphan mindset is rooted in Men of God that have chosen to abandon their role as, not just mentors, but true fathers. They have inadvertently contributed to the rise of a love-starved, directionless generation of believers that live in a famine mentality, starving for fathers.

At the beginning of 2017 Terry had just completed a forty-day fast. He was seeking guidance from God for the direction of the upcoming year, when the Lord began to drop words into his spirit. The Lord spoke these words to Terry: "I'm bringing a shaking to the church and I will separate the Lots from the Abrahams, those who seek me and not just my blessings." We will elaborate on this later in the book.

The Lord also came to Ren a few years back and spoke to him revealing God's plan to bring a shaking on the earth. It moved pastor Ren to write a song titled, *Shake the Earth*. This shaking will bring about a recalibration of God's church. It's a realignment of His children into a lean mean army for the Lord that can carry out the task of stewarding revival. It's a shifting of perspective back to a truth in the word of God that has been submerged for far too long, a truth the church needs to hear if we are ever to walk in the legacy and fullness of our inheritance. That truth is found in scripture.

> *And he will turn the hearts of fathers to their children and the hearts of children to their fathers, lest I come and strike the land with a decree of utter destruction* (Malachi 4:6).

We have reaped a generation that has faced utter destruction but the Lord is willing to bring about that destruction for our benefit. The word here for "utter destruction" in the Hebrew is the same as "a day set aside for destruction." God is willing to bring us to a precipice in order that our eyes might open and see the cliff that the church and our world is headed over. We believe it's not too late; it's not too far gone. The church needs to lead the way and sound the alarm.

Arise fathers and turn the hearts of sons! For sonship does not exist without fathers. Just as we are called to be sons of God, we are also called to be sons of godly fathers; but we have had a void of fathers raising sons. We live in a bankrupt generation, a generation of fatherlessness in the natural world. Is it possible that this natural manifestation is rooted in the supernatural abandonment of spiritual fathers? Is it possible that the cure for this fatherless generation is for a rise and positioning of spiritual fathers to step in, step up and teach our generation of Christ followers how to become sons and how to grow into fathers?

We are going to take you on a journey of discovery that shows you the impact that spiritual leaders have on all of us. We will show you the ultimate outcome of how fathers impacted, mentored, and discipled those in their charge and influence. You'll see both the good and the ugly – those that mentored correctly and those that derailed generations by not raising them up in the way they should go. We read in the book of Proverbs that fathers are to raise up children in the way they should go (Proverbs 22:6). This applies to our mentors and spiritual fathers, too. But that task is impossible if Malachi 4:6 is not followed and honored. Your heart must beat for those you're raising. We need a generation of pastors, leaders, and Jesus followers to take up the call. This generation cannot navigate the waters of this world without loving spiritual parents taking over, committed to seeing their sons succeed and inherit everything God has stored up for them.

Both Terry and Ren understand what it means to have fathers that leave holes in them from abandonment. We both had fathers that would disappear for long periods, sometimes years and then randomly show up in our lives again, only to leave again and add to our Swiss cheese identity. The holes needed to be filled and both of us filled those holes through worldly encounters until Father God plucked us out of their lostness. On the other hand, we both had encounters with God where He spoke clearly to us that He Himself would be our Father and raise us up to be godly men.

We are going to teach you what God Himself taught us. We are going to release this generational blessing of spiritual fathering that will outlast your lifetime. If done by God's plan, this will release a 1000-generational blessing in your life. We believe that this revelation holds the key to breaking the bastard spirit along with two other spirits you will learn about later in the book: the famine spirit and the poverty spirit. By breaking off these spirits, we will see ministers, leaders, business entrepreneurs and servants that are able to fully walk out the calling on their life.

We are filling in the missing pieces of the body of Christ, helping equip the church to be an example to the world and groom the bride of Christ into her fullness. The shaking of the church has begun to disrupt the old conflict-ridden system. The shaking reveals dissatisfaction with the current way that the church leadership is run. We are not writing this book to tear down churches or leaders. Quite the contrary, we desire to build up churches by using what we have learned from being fatherless and finding a Father.

Just as every natural child resembles their natural parents, so do we reflect the image of God. We are image bearers, created in His likeness. There are three parts to our God. Father, Son and His Holy Spirit. We have entered into a decade of the church moving into sonship. We talk about being good sons. We write books about sonship, teach seminars and help sons feel like our Father loves us. We identify with our likeness of Jesus as a Son but the church has yet to identify with our likeness of the Father. We are called to be fathers. If we bear the image of the Father, then we should also be fathers. We can not fully bear the Father's image when we do not yet do what He does. Be a father.

We are going to walk you down this road of understanding how to father so the church can truly make disciples and raise up a strong generation to lead us into revival. To do this, we have to first know our enemy. What is Satan's strategy and what tools is he using to barricade the door that opens to our full inheritance? We are going to learn to recognize the red flags, the enemy's banner. We are going to closely exam the critical roles fathers play in our spiritual growth and victories, how fathers equip us for our callings. We are going to learn from the biblical fathers God has given us as a narrative from which we can absorb truth. We are going to unlock the revelation of successful fathering and the power it has to turn the tide of a son's destiny from a tale of warning to a tale of triumph. You are going to be able to step out and father in your Father's image. It's time to unlock this mystery of being a spiritual father and defeat this bastard spirit whose mission is to stop you.

This book doesn't target what made sons broken, it targets what is making fathers break sons. This demonic mandate loves watching the very people entrusted by God to raise up the next generation cripple them instead. We are going to dismantle this dark force and set captive fathers free.

Pray this prayer with us: Father God, as I read this book, Lord, open my eyes to see all that You are revealing. Make me aware of the revelations unfolding before me. Lord, I pray Malachi 4:6, that you turn the hearts of the fathers to their children and the hearts of the children to their fathers. And Father, if there is anything within me as I read this book that needs to be revealed in my life, Lord reveal all of it. Stir my heart toward You in a new way. I open up my heart to You, Lord; make me more like You. In Jesus' name. Amen.

CHAPTER 1

WHAT IS THE BASTARD SPIRIT?

What an inflammatory title we have come up with! Many of you may have heard of the orphan spirit. Some have made the case that it's actually a mindset and not a spirit. Whether we are talking about a spirit or mindset is not really our issue. We've labeled this a spirit to help identify the demonic assignment that creates a mindset in saints to believe they have valueless sons. This, in turn, cultivates an environment for sons to feel valueless in the kingdom.

The definition of the noun "bastard" in the Webster's Dictionary is "an illegitimate son," defined as follows.

The noun use of bastard is defined as: "an illegitimate son."

One of Webster's definitions of the adjective of "bastard" is: "lacking genuineness or authority."

Many would call a child born out of wedlock or a son born out of an affair a bastard. He is born under less than pure circumstances and can carry a stain or disdain by his parents or the community. Ren's mother was born out of an affair. For years, she was severely beaten as a child because she was a constant reminder to her mother of her own sinful act. She was seen as illegitimate by her mother and suffered wounds to her identity and her soul as a result of things that she had no say in. She was not treated the same as the "legitimate" children, those born in wedlock.

So a bastard is not a bad word. It is a son whose father is robbing him of his ability to be seen by his father as worthy, as a legitimate heir, which leaves the son void of his father's authority.

The Fatherlessness Agenda

We call this demonic mandate "the fatherlessness agenda." This seeps not just into your mind but clouds your spirit in brokenness. Our fathers who carry a bastard spirit or bastard mindset, however you want to define it, are those that cannot see how mentoring the next generation is crucial for raising up powerful and healthy men and women of God. So they partner in relationships with leadership as long as those under them walk as a bond servant or a friend but never allow them to become sons.

The bastard spirit creates competition between spiritual sons and fathers. Fathers are fighting for territory and believing that everyone out there will take away their piece of the pie.

Spiritual sons are a threat to the father's own success and are perceived as throne usurpers. They are made to feel as if they are stealing the authority of their father's own kingdom as they believe they are unloved or unworthy enough to be given territory and authority in their own right.

The most insidious assignment and goal of the bastard spirit is to destroy the ability to understand the Father's love. So, by creating a fatherlessness mindset in you, the enemy can then increase the chances of creating an orphan mindset in the next generation. Fathers who create orphans have no heirs. It is not okay for you to remain without heirs.

A mistaken notion of God

An example that happened to pastor Terry was early in his ministry. He had started to become highly frustrated with a series of financial and spiritual problems that never seemed to come to resolution. The frustration always appeared towards a spiritual leader who demanded so much loyalty and honor but never gave any form of covenantal relationship (sonship). The problems associated with the frustration he felt began affecting his personal life and even caused problems within his marriage and friendships. Finally, Terry sought counseling to help him cope.

One day during the counseling session, Terry walked into the room, fell on the couch and began to cry, "I feel like my Heavenly Father is like my real dad. He lives far away and shows up once a year with a nice gift. He'll spend a couple days with me and says He loves me but then He leaves me here to be abused when He could come rescue me." It was at that moment he knew why he was struggling. He saw His Heavenly Father through the lens of the bastard spirit his biological father had released. Terry's father treating him like an illegitimate son had created seeping wounds in Terry's soul. Those wounds caused a blockade around Terry. Unable to move past them, he was incapable of reproducing healthy spiritual sons.

Hence, the bastard spirit is an epidemic that seeks to sterilize the healthy spiritual reproduction of the next generation of leaders. We learn in basic biology that all healthy organisms reproduce. This spirit attacks right at the heart of Father God's first commandment: "Be fruitful and multiply!"

> *And God blessed them. And God said to them, "Be fruitful and multiply and fill the earth and subdue it, and have dominion over the fish of the sea and over the birds of the heavens and over every living thing that moves on the earth" (Genesis 1:28).*

Research 'subdue'

The bastard spirit in fathers

You see, this bastard spirit cleaves, creates and causes. The bastard spirit cleaves to fathers and creates behaviors in the fathers that cause sons to feel illegitimate. The sons believe they are powerless and carry no authority. Subordinate leaders feel they are followers because of the personalities of the senior leaders above them, and settle into the role of employees who have no authority. Some of our pastors have created "staff members" and not sons. If you don't perform, you are fired and the relationship comes to an end. Now pastors, you don't have to keep every worker – not everyone will remain in your care. But while they are, it is crucial to cultivate an image of value and godly authority inside of them.

Many churches have also been walking in the bastard spirit. Even church boards have bastardized our senior pastors in many churches. The senior pastor is seen as a hireling that must perform according to their expectations to have value and authority, or the board will vote on whether he can keep his job. Since when did we let sons decide what fathers can and cannot correct? I wonder if Saul would have fired Samuel for correcting him and telling him he couldn't be king. Boards are not the priest. Business leaders are not the pastor and they have no business controlling the prophet's tongue. If Saul's court, as the employer, would have had a vote on who should be priest, he would have placed Eli as priest since Eli would not have brought correction on Saul just as Eli did not bring correction on his own sons.

The bastard spirit reduces sons to nothing more than employees.

You can fire your sons who work for you but, even if they don't work for you, they still stay your sons. If your value to a leader is tied to your title or role, then you are not a son. The bastard spirit ties your sonship to servanthood. If you're not serving at their level of expectation, then you have no value and your relationship status is terminated with your employment status.

It's also important to understand that the bastard spirit robs you of a kingdom mindset. Someone who walks in the kingdom mindset is focused on legacy and doing the will of God: "Thy kingdom come, thy will be done" (Matthew 6:10). We are ambassadors of the kingdom of God; therefore everything we do should be for the growth of God's kingdom and not ours.

Fear of competition

One of the key characteristics of the bastard spirit is competition that is motivated strictly by fear or pride. The bastard mindset makes fathers believe that, if their sons rise up and become more popular or have more resources, then the fathers will have less. The flipside is actually true. The more your sons grow and grow the kingdom, the bigger will your God-given legacy grow and the bigger your win. We are all on the same team. We are all citizens of heaven. Therefore, when heaven wins, all of us win!

It's crazy to think that there are fathers who feel so threatened and challenged by the potential success of their sons that they would begin to compete and even become jealous. **Your competition and your jealousy are actually warring against yourself and potentially holding up your legacy from growing.**

A mind boggling example found in the Old Testament is the fact that even after David marries King Saul's daughter and is a member of his family, Saul still feels threatened by David's success. He is now a son-in-law, a legal heir to the throne. He should be rejoicing over David but instead he just can't keep that song that's stuck in his head from playing: the song the women sang as they danced, and said: "Saul has slain his thousands and David his ten thousands" (1 Samuel 18:7).

Yet David's only motive was to serve the king and serve him well to grow his kingdom. The reason David walked like this is because Samuel operated in the spirit of the father and poured his anointing on him so that David could walk in the Father spirit of God. David's presence in the house of Saul meant that the house of Saul would be prosperous and have an incredible legacy but the bastard spirit in Saul blinded him to the true status of things and sent him into a murderous rage.

Fathers who compete with their children from a place of jealousy and do not want to better their sons will eventually wound their sons and send them on the run to other kingdoms.

Then David said in his heart, "Now I shall perish one day by the hand of Saul. There is nothing better for me than that I should escape to the land of the Philistines. Then Saul will despair of seeking me any longer within the borders of Israel, and I shall escape out of his hand." So David arose and went over, he and the six hundred men who were with him, to Achish the son of Maoch, king of Gath (1 Samuel 27:1-2).

Note that, when Saul attacked David, David went on the run and eventually even began to exercise his identity to add to the kingdom of the Philistines. David used his ability to help them become successful, not because he was angry at Saul but because of Saul's rejection of him. I wonder how many of our sons who should be growing God's kingdom, have been rejected and are now making the enemy prosperous and growing the kingdom of darkness?

Church leaders need to be mindful of the fact that they're not just building a pulpit for one decade but a legacy for generations to come.

This legacy can only be possible by having children who can carry it on.

> *Behold, children are a heritage from the Lord, the fruit of the womb, a reward. Like arrows in the hand of a warrior are the children of one's youth. Blessed is the man who fills his quiver with them! He shall not be put to shame when he speaks with his enemies in the gate* (Psalm 127:3-5).

This is yet another reason why the bastard spirit wants to separate sons from fathers. Re-read Psalm 127:5: "*Blessed is the man who fills his quiver with them! He shall not be put to shame when he speaks with his enemies in the gate.*" A father with no sons will be in a weakened state when he tries to stand against the enemy, whereas the father who has many sons can stand boldly in the knowledge that he has built up a warrior tribe ready for spiritual warfare. How much more powerful would our churches be today, if there were fathers and sons united in one heart!

This might be a good time to mention that a quiver has a set number of arrows that can be put into it, so fathers do need to be careful of how many sons they bring on. Don't bring on more sons than you can raise. Once sons become fathers, you can then add more sons. When sons transform from sons to fathers, they are transformed from arrows to quivers – as arrows leave your quiver it allows more room for more sons to be added. This means a good father will never hold on to an arrow because what good is an arrow that's not been released? Even business leaders understand that the core of a business franchise is to create more copies of you. If a quiver holds twelve and the twelve become fathers with quivers of their own, there are now 156 arrows.

False identity
The bastard spirit wants to undermine and destroy the life-giving role of the father and give a false identity to the next generation of leaders. To understand the bastard spirit fully, we need to understand what it is warring against. What does a father give and what does the bastard spirit try to take away? We need to contrast the two.

The bastard spirit causes sons to fear the voice of men over the voice of God.

*Saul said to Samuel, "I have sinned, for I have transgressed the commandment of the Lord and your words, because **I feared the people and obeyed their voice**"* (1 Samuel 15:24 , emphasis added).

The Fruit of the Bastard Spirit
The fruit of the bastard spirits are illegitimate sons that rise into illegitimate nations. A single seed allowed to sprout has wreaked havoc on whole regions, nations and historical time periods. We have to understand the nefarious goals of the enemy. When the enemy is successful in creating illegitimate sons, he strategically uses them to target the sons he was unsuccessful in accosting, the promise carriers of God. The illegitimate sons form nations, and those nations become those that taunt and try to derail the true children of God.

Consider the following facts in bible history:

- The Canaanites and Hitties are both the illegitimate descendants of Ham, who made himself an "illegitimate" son of Noah. We will expand more on this later in the book.
- The Arabic nations that led to Islam were the ancestors of Ishmael, the illegitimate son of Abraham.
- The Moabites and Ammonites were the ancestors of Ammon and Moab, the illegitimate children of Lot's daughters after they slept with their father Lot.
- The Amalekites were the descendants of Amalek, the son of Eliphaz and his concubine. Eliphaz was the son of Esau. Esau was brother to Jacob and the son who lost his standing as a first son and hated Jacob and his sons because of his fall from being the heir of Isaac.

However, it is wrong to assume that illegitimacy automatically breeds dishonorable offspring. Perez, who was one of the twins of an incestuous union between Tamar and her father-in-law Judah, grew up to override his circumstances and become a man of honor (Genesis 38:27-30). Amazingly, Perez is recorded as the ancestor of David from whose line came Jesus the Messiah (Matthew 1:3-16).

The point we are making here is the perception of being spiritually illegitimate. For spiritually illegitimate sons will always fight a ministry or organization for its promised land. Producing illegitimate sons will always cause battles to your legacy you don't want to have to fight.

We want to make it clear that, no matter how great a spiritual father you are, illegitimate sons are inevitable. If you raise up many leaders, you will have some that just refuse correction and stray off the path. Isaac was a good father and still had an Esau that did not value his birthright. If Isaac isn't a good enough example, let me give you one that is not disputable. Judas had the best teacher, preacher, mentor and spiritual father you could ask for. Jesus was perfect and still had an illegitimate son in Judas. The question of whether or not a spiritual father is under the bastard spirit is not whether or not an illegitimate son is produced but whether or not that is the pattern. You need to ask if this is a pattern, and if it is, you need to have the maturity to see what role you are playing in that production.

CHAPTER 2

DEFINING FATHERS AND SONS

"Before you become a leader, success is all about growing
yourself. When you become a leader, success is all about
growing others."
~ Jack Welch

This concept that we are defining of fathers and sons in the
Old Testament is mirrored in the New Testament as the term
"disciples." So why not just use the terms "teacher" and "disciple"?
Because our limited understanding of what a disciple truly looked
like, I mean, the Jesus model of discipleship, is so misunderstood.
Discipleship digs so much deeper than just simple education by
a teacher passing information that just dropping that label would
be a grave injustice of your ability to catch what we are releasing.

Jesus' Model of Discipling

So let's dig into what discipleship in Jesus' day looked like. Jesus
was called "Rabbi," which literally translates as "Teacher." It was
the job of the rabbis to educate the next generation being raised
up. The rabbis would select students for a variety of reasons.
These students were called *Talmidim* (*talmid*, singular) in Hebrew,
which is translated as "disciples."

17

The discipleship in the church model of Jesus' day was truly a model of fathers making sons who became fathers. As the rabbis would teach them, the disciples' goal was not just to learn from their teacher to get the grade or degree, but to truly become like their teacher in every way possible. The rabbi and the disciple both had the same desire: as best they could, the disciple would become the image of the teacher. They modeled this after the God of creation who made man in His image (Genesis 1:27).

The rabbi would interview and ultimately select students that exhibited qualities that best convinced him that these young men could someday model and reflect the image of the rabbi. They did everything their rabbi did; they went everywhere the rabbi went. When the rabbi was convinced that they had become like him in every way possible, he sent them out to go and repeat the process of making disciples that, in turn, would look like the junior rabbi as well. When you arrived at the age of thirty, you were permitted to then take on disciples. This insured that sons were given time to be properly raised up and that fathers had time to raise them. Then the cycle was to be repeated.

Jesus modeled the role of a spiritual father perfectly within the setting of the spiritual system of Israel. They understood the significance of the spiritual father and son role. In our time, we must return to a Jesus modeled environment of making disciples in light of the rabbi's understanding. Their model was to take the young ones and replicate their spiritual DNA in them and have them do the same with spiritual grandsons. They spoke life into them while they were in a season that was the most receptive in their stage of life.

We can do the same! Paul echoed this narrative that simply being a guide was not enough when he spoke about how he had fathered those in Corinth.

I do not write these things to make you ashamed, but to admonish you as my beloved children. For though you have countless guides in Christ, you do not have many fathers. For I became your father in Christ Jesus through the gospel. I urge you, then, be imitators of me (1 Corinthians 4:14-16).

We want to make it understood from the outset that as we are using the term "son," in a generic sense, and not necessarily attributing gender to it. We do believe that the father and the mother in the natural world are each crucial to the healthy upbringing of both sons and daughters. They each have their own irreplaceable roles in children's lives. A natural mother cannot replace the role of a natural father in a son or daughter and vice versa. When we are discussing spiritual sons, we do recognize that this role can be filtered through what Paul wrote in Galatians:

There is neither Jew nor Gentile, neither slave nor free, nor is there male and female, for you are all one in Christ Jesus. If you belong to Christ, then you are Abraham's seed, and heirs according to the promise (Galatians 3:28-29 NIV).

In the spiritual sense, we believe that mentors and leaders can come in both male and female form and both are heirs to the promise. We both are of the belief that women are totally free to serve in all roles of leadership. That said, it's important for both our fathers and mothers to assume the right roles in raising both our sons and daughters. Our encouragement to female senior pastors is this. Find a father in your house that will fill his role of raising spiritual sons and daughters from the dad's unique qualifications. Male senior pastors, find a spiritual mother in your house that will fill the role of raising up spiritual sons and daughters from the mom's unique qualifications. So, for the rest of this book you will mainly see us reference sons and daughters as sons only – but you can apply either. Hey, just think about it this way. If we as men have to be brides and wear a wedding dress, then you ladies can be hairy sons!

One of the reasons we believe that writing in particular about fathers is that we are in a time when it seems we are facing fatherlessness more than ever. The role of a father is irreplaceable especially in the role of spiritual fathers. Statistics from Focus on the Family Publishing, "Promise Keepers at Work" show this in a staggering way. If a child is the first person in a household to become a Christian, there is a 3.5 percent probability everyone else in the household will follow. If the mother is the first to become a Christian, there is a 17 percent probability everyone else in the household will follow. But if the father is the first, there is a 93 percent probability everyone else in the household will follow. We cannot just ignore that! According to data collected by Promise Keepers and Baptist Press, if a father does not go to church, even if his wife does, only one child in fifty will become a regular worshiper.

Folks, we need to reach fathers and, to do so, we need spiritual fathers to stand up and report for duty. It's time for our men to raise up a generation of strong sons and daughters who know their identity in Christ and will raise up the next generation. **He who has a father has a future.**

Prodigal Sons and Fathers

We now live in a generation where we are discovering our Doctor Huxtables are actually Bill Cosbys! We are watching many fathers fall at a rapid rate and other fathers refuse to step up to the positions they are called to. Now we have sons who would never even get the chance to become prodigals because they have never had fathers to begin with. We are a bastardized generation. So the question we are asking is what do we do about this?

We believe part of the answer can be found in Jesus' story of The Prodigal Son. The father in this parable is a radical example of what this generation needs in leaders. The son goes to his father and basically says, "I wish you were dead so that I can have my inheritance." The father makes a painful sacrifice and allows him to make a huge mistake. He's willing to release his son in great pain and mourn him. The father sells part of his own estate, thereby selling his ability at future livelihood to make sure his son can have the inheritance now. Understand that by selling his estate is likened to him to selling his factory which is an income generator. All of this after his son had dishonored him. Then the father watches the son go and live in the world. However, the father, regardless of his son's actions, never gives up on the son. We know this because Jesus says that, when the son finally comes back home to the father, the father is looking out for him from afar off. Every day he is waiting and watching. Let's pick up the story in Luke starting with verse 17.

> *"But when he came to himself, he said, 'How many of my father's hired servants have more than enough bread, but I perish here with hunger! I will arise and go to my father, and I will say to him, "Father, I have sinned against heaven and before you. I am no longer worthy to be called your son. Treat me as one of your hired servants"'"* (Luke 15:17-19).

So as the son returns home and his father reaches him, he begins to give the speech he has carefully rehearsed:

"And the son said to him, 'Father, I have sinned against heaven and before you. I am no longer worthy to be called your son.' But the father said to his servants, 'Bring quickly the best robe, and put it on him, and put a ring on his hand, and shoes on his feet. And bring the fattened calf and kill it, and let us eat and celebrate. For this my son was dead, and is alive again; he was lost, and is found.' And they began to celebrate" (Luke 15:21-24).

Look at what the father does. He doesn't just cut off the son's rehearsed speech but he flat out ignores his attempt at presenting a diminished image of himself. As soon as he says he is unworthy to be called a son, the father begins his work of fully restoring him and providing for him by calling for his servants to bring his image back.

The father gives the son back his destiny. How? First, the father puts his best robe on him. The son feels unworthy and unrighteous to be considered a son but the father covers his unrighteousness of filthy rags with the garments of salvation, the robe of righteousness, (Isaiah 61:10). This is the same thing that Christ does for us (Galatians 3:27). Next he places a signet ring on him. Why is this significant? All through the Old Testament we see signet rings as a symbol of authority. Rings were not typically worn as jewelry but they were identification symbols of the authority of the house (the family name) and giving it represented a commitment to the son. Rings were seals used to sign official letters. The son now officially has the authority of his father's house.

The father then gives him shoes. All throughout Old Testament history, slaves, captives, and servants did not wear shoes. But sons did! The father is saying, "You are not a servant; you are a son!" By giving him shoes, he was giving him identity and status. Removing shoes was also a sign of mourning. We see King David covering his head and removing his shoes after the death of his son, Absalom (2 Samuel 15:30). Similarly, the prophet Ezekiel is instructed not to weep or remove his shoes after his wife dies (Ezekiel 24:17). So what is the prodigal's father saying? He is saying, "Our time of mourning is over because you have come home and you no longer are a servant to another master: you are my son!"

Then the father, who already sacrificed for him before he left, is willingly sacrificing more of what he owns to celebrate his son's homecoming. Jesus is our sacrifice. His sacrifice is for the atonement of sins: it is the price of our rebellion. Our Heavenly Father received us in and sacrificed Jesus for reconciliation as a celebration of our return home. **And, while we were still unworthy to untie his sandals, Jesus washed our feet clean and put shoes on our feet fitted with the readiness that comes from the gospel of peace** (Ephesians 6:15).

So the father covers his son's sin (robe), He gives him back his authority (ring), and he is no longer a servant but a restored son (shoes). He completes the restoration and makes payment (fatted calf). These are the same steps our Father in heaven takes with our own lives when we come back into relationship with Him. There is no doubt at this point that he is forgiven.

While this story is about prodigal sons, we face an unprecedented time where we encounter a counter culture of prodigal fathers. We have prodigal fathers who have sold the farm out from underneath their sons, with no intention of leaving inheritance or legacy. The fathers have physically and spiritually checked out of their sons' lives. So now we have sons with no fathers to return home to and we are wondering why our generation has broken out in violence and is directionless. We are calling for "prodigal fathers" to return home and for fatherless sons to step into the role of being spiritual fathers.

CHAPTER 3

THE ROLES OF THE FATHER: NAME-GIVER AND PROVIDER

I will tell of the decree:
The LORD SAID TO ME, "YOU ARE MY SON;
today I have begotten you.
Ask of me, and I will make the nations your heritage,
and the ends of the earth your possession"
(Psalm 2:7-8).

The Father is a name-giver, provider, prophet, priest, and king of the home. As a provider, He gives you access to inheritance. As a prophet, He has the ability to speak to His son's destiny. As a priest, He has the right to give His son blessing. And as a king, He has the position to decree His son's authority. When a father abandons his son, he limits his rights and is merely a DNA giver. So, while a spiritual father can never give physical DNA, he can provide multiple roles for the son to be empowered.

In the next few chapters we will look further into the Father's roles of Name-Giver, Provider, Prophet, Priest and King and their tremendous significance for His sons.

Name-Giver

First, the father gives his son a name. The last name carries the history and legacy of the family, while the first name carries identity and destiny.

Ren's father waited for a few weeks after he was born to give him a name. His reason? He wanted to get to know his personality and give him a name that fit him. When Ren was born, he was six pounds seven ounces but the doctors did not believe that was possible, given his tiny stature. He fit in his mom's shoe box as a three-month-old. The doctors thought he could not be over four pounds at birth. They took him to three scales because they assumed the first two were broken. On the third scale he stood up on the scale with only the need for a nurse to balance him. He had enough strength in his legs to stay upright. So, after seeing his small beginning size and the strength he showed through the first weeks, his father named him "Ren," meaning, "little, mighty, and powerful." His name spoke identity over him.

Ren's name also got him his wife. Yes, that's right: it was the direct contributor to him meeting his wife. He was at a Christian concert and someone was amazed when he heard his name and said, "Your name is Ren? Have you met the other Ren – she's a girl?" Turns out Ren's wife Rachael was close friends with this other friend and, while Ren was humoring the banter about the two Rens, he had already fallen hard for Rachael. Love at first sight! Without his name he might have missed his wife!

Your name has more value than you think.

Names given in the bible have two components. There is the birth name which often represents the recipient's identity. The word that we translate as "name" in Hebrew is *shem*. The English word "name" does not do justice to the depth of the Hebrew counterpart.

Shem is much more about one's identity within a community than just identification.

Imagine someone walking up to you and, instead of simply asking what your name is and you answering, "Bill," you are being asked, "What is your identity?" It speaks to your education, your status, your station, your skills, attributes and authority. To come in one's name in biblical times is literally to come in one's given authority. A soldier may say to a thief, "Stop in the name of the king!" This means the soldier is operating under the king's authority and represents his power and identity as he invokes his name. Similarly, a messenger comes in the name of the message sender, not in his own authority. The message sent has the full weight of the sender, not the deliverer. First names always carry their owner's authority; last names or family names always carry their father's authority.

That's why it is so important that we grasp the significance of using Jesus' name. "In Jesus name" is not a complimentary close to your prayer but rather stating in whose authority you have spoken. You come in the name (the authority) of the King of Kings, Yeshua, Son of God, and in His authority have you made these decrees.

Even in recent modern times, identity has been found in names. The last name "Baker" was because the family were originally actual culinary bakers. The name "Ward" was originally associated with a watchmen or guard. The name "Smith" was originally one who worked with metals, such as a blacksmith.

Names carry identity. Are you catching it yet? That's why in the bible after the angel declares to Mary that she will have a son, he tells her what her son, the Savior's name would be –

Jesus (Matthew 1:31). We find out that not only is His name Jesus but Isaiah 9:6 tells us He will be called "Wonderful Counselor, Mighty God, Everlasting Father, Prince of Peace." These names give identity. But let's look at Jesus' actual name. The modern transliteration of the Messiah's name is not exactly how He would have heard His name spoken in His day. The Hebrew version of "Jesus" that He would have been called growing up would have been *Yeshua bar Yosef*, translated, "Joshua son of Joseph." Yes "Joshua" was the more correct transliteration of His name than our modern Jesus pronunciation; but I don't believe He minds our rendition of "Jesus." So, we will just stay with "Jesus." He knows full well who we are talking about.

In biblical times you were identified with your name followed by your father's name. Most of us are aware that Jesus didn't have the last name "Christ." "Christ" was the Greek term for the Hebrew equivalent of Messiah (the Anointed One), meaning Savior. So He would have had the Hebrew name/title *Yeshua Hamashiach* (Jesus the Messiah). But, if you were really wanting to properly identify His true identity, you would have called him Yeshua bar Yahweh (Jesus Son of God). His name holds His authority, and all of the names we call Him, including the transliteration of Jesus, all have the power of His authority. God gave Him His name and placed the Father's authority in it. **A father's job is to give his son his name that will carry his authority in it.**

Ren's oldest son, Isaiah, is at Randy Clark's ministry school now and people will always come up to him when they find out his last name, Schuffman. They ask if he is the son of Ren. He calls Ren all the time to tell him how his name opens opportunities for ministry for him, opportunities to meet and talk to the speakers that Ren knows and has relationships with. He gets an opportunity to climb higher than his father. Ren's youngest son Caleb told his father one night, "Dad, I'm going to go even higher in ministry than you because you have let me stand on your shoulders."

That's it! A father allows his sons to use his name to multiply the authority he carries. That is why a son will be worried about failure because it will tarnish the family name as well as the authority of the name he was given.

The scriptures are chock full of names holding significance, for God clearly values names –

especially new names that He gives, too. In so many stories you see God take an active role in the naming and renaming process. Jacob becomes Israel, Abram becomes Abraham, Sarai becomes Sarah. God changes their name to fit the identity that God sees and decrees into them. When God changed someone's name in the bible, it was usually to establish a new identity and to reflect prophetic destiny. When God changed Abram's name to Abraham and Sarai's name to Sarah, He declared that their barrenness had ended and added the Hebrew letter "*hey*" to their name. The "*hey*" (the breath of His presence within His Name) was added to theirs. "*Hey*" means "breath" or "behold," as if looking in awe upon a great sight. Behold God's covenant, His very breath, was added to Abraham's identity.

> *Then he said, "Your name shall no longer be called Jacob, but Israel, for you have striven with God and with men, and have prevailed"* (Genesis 32:28).

Jacob's name means "supplanter" or "trickster." God then changed his name to give him a new identity. **He is no longer his past but has been given a future.** From now on every time someone calls him "Israel," they are declaring he is an overcomer, one who prevails. This reinforces his character and now speaks life.

God follows this model with reference to Himself as well. Every time He reveals Himself in Genesis, we see Him introduce Himself with a new name. In the first chapter He is *Elohim* "God at a distance." In the second chapter He is *Yahweh,* the personal name of God. Later we meet him as *Adonai* meaning "Lord" or "Master." As the chapters unfold, He begins to establish His characteristics. When Abraham calls God "*Jehovah-Jireh,*" he is saying, "the Lord will Provide," extending the character of God to a provider.

God uses the same model for Jesus. ... "*and his name shall be called Wonderful Counselor, Mighty God, Everlasting Father, Prince of Peace*" (Isaiah 9:6). Since a name speaks identity and destiny, God named Jesus with something that would show the world His character, identity, purpose and destiny. The Hebrew name "*Yeshua*" means "salvation." Interestingly, it is the only biblical name that is interchangeable with its biblical word, so when you see the word "salvation" in the Old Testament, it is usually the Hebrew word "*Yeshua*"! God wants to give you a new name as well.

What identity did for Ren

In the spring of 2006, Ren was high up in the Colorado mountains. It was late one evening and he decided to spend some time walking along the banks of a small nearby lake in quiet prayer. It was void of any of man's light or pollution. This high up and this far out from any towns or population made the night sky come to life in the beautifully contrasted darkness. Every star was bold and bright. Ren had taken a retreat to the mountains to help him process one of the most difficult seasons of his life. There was never a season he felt so defeated and rejected. His wife had left him and his future was uncertain. Having life-long father issues and now marriage issues left him on rocky ground as to his own identity.

29

Walking around and praying Ren was suddenly overcome by God's creation. He lay down along the bank and stared up at the radiant night sky. As he lay there, he began to start a conversation with God. "God, how do You see me; what is my name?" This was the question burning on his heart.

To his astonishment the Lord answered clearly, "You are My David."

"David?" Ren questioned confused and excited. Why would the Lord call him David?

The Lord answered once again. "David was a king: you are My leader."

"Yeah that is true," Ren thought.

"David was a psalmist: you are my musician," the Lord continued.

Ren had been a worship leader since 1996, so that was accurate as well.

"You are not afraid of any giants," God said.

Ren grew up in LA and faced aggression constantly. He had been shot at, stabbed, robbed at gunpoint, all without carrying any of the trauma that should have come from it.

Finally, the Lord paused and then declared, "You have a heart after Mine like David."

At that, Ren wept. That moment would become a measuring rod for him that would define his call. It was his burning bush encounter. God shifted him from his wandering into his pursuit of purpose.

When you hear the name the Lord calls you, something shifts inside of you. Most people are terrified to ask God this question because they are terrified of God's response. Sons who have faced abandonment and are hounded by the bastard spirit usually fear that, if asked, they will hear that they are wicked and valueless in God's eyes. They are haunted by their own insecurities so that they expect to be found wanting for value. This is NEVER the truth. When you ask God to show you your name and your identity, He will always answer you with what He wants you to become, not where you are at the moment. God wants you to see what's possible for your future.

Your name carries your plan and purpose.

The name and description of David was able to help Ren anchor every storm in his life after this moment. No longer did he have to suffer the bastard spirit's assault on his identity. Over the next decade and a half, many people would try to speak death over his identity; but every time Ren was able to return back to the word of the Lord and declare, "Those words about my character are void because they do not line up with what God said about me."

Your name gives you a measuring rod for how you are walking out your calling. If Ren was not living up to the version of himself that God saw, Ren would simply have said, "That is not the heart David had after God," or "David wasn't afraid of this battle." He would not have encouraged himself in the Lord to rise up to who he really was.

Now, armed with a sense of who he was in the Lord, the assaults against his heart would fall to the ground like water off a duck's back. The test of this was the character assassination attempts coming from people he loved and whose opinion he cared deeply about. However, knowing David faced the same assault on his heart, allowed Ren to lean into that model and walk out his own struggle.

The Lord has sought for Himself a man after His own heart, and the Lord has commanded him to be commander over His people...(1 Samuel 13:14 NKJV)

After God says David has a heart like His and is the reason why he is chosen to lead, David experiences just the opposite. When David was sent to the battlefront to take his brothers some food, he sees what is happening with Goliath, and he inquires of it.

Now Eliab his eldest brother heard when he spoke to the men. And Eliab's anger was kindled against David, and he said, "Why have you come down? And with whom have you left those few sheep in the wilderness? I know your presumption and the evil of your heart, for you have come down to see the battle." And David said, "What have I done now? Was it not but a word?" And he turned away from him toward another, and spoke in the same way, and the people answered him again as before (1 Samuel 17:28-30).

David's own brother assaults David's heart! He calls it evil. He assaults his value with the "few sheep" comment. How many times have pastors been caught in misplaced identity because of the few sheep in the church we shepherd! Your few paycheck dollars or your small business, are the few sheep that the enemy likes to ridicule. We think that is our failed identity instead of realizing we are one Goliath away from our promotion. David, like Ren, had the truth about his heart spoken over him, so when his brother comes against it, David quickly dismisses the accusation before it can steal David's moment.

Let me translate David's response. "Bro, what's your deal? I just made one statement." David rolls his eyes and goes back to his conversation which would lead to his moment to show his warrior identity.

The bastard spirit is on a mission to steal your name. **The enemy wants to blot out your name so he can block out your future.** He wants to steal your identity from you. Bastards do not carry their father's last name. They are not "the son of." Only a legitimate heir is allowed to carry the name of their father. If you don't have his name, then you don't have his authority.

Fathers, when you treat your son as a bastard, you are taking your identity off them and removing your authority. Our spiritual fathers have to give sons their name. Even more than their own name, spiritual fathers need to help sons find the name God gives them. You need to know your name, and you need to know how God sees you! This is not optional! His word about you will always carry more weight than the lies of the enemy. Need identity? You have not because you ask not. Stop fearing His reply!

Not the brand but the person

In Psalm 27:4 we learned that it was necessary to duplicate the arrows and quivers that God gives us. But what the church has done is to make a grievous mistake about what duplication looks like. Pastors and leaders think they need to duplicate their church brand, when what they really need to do is duplicate their church sons. They're too busy trying to open up more buildings with their name on them instead of sons with their name in them.

Franchises are always aided by the name but they are not necessarily successful just because of the name. I have seen one franchise becoming successful while the other one fails, even though they both carry the same name and are in identical demographics. No, the ultimate success of one franchise over another is the person running the franchise. The difference can be the DNA of the person in the leadership position. A strong name coupled with a leader that has been duplicated will always replicate the success of the original. The best franchises don't just give you their business name; they send you through training to create the same leadership skills, the same heart, the same mentality and commitment as the original. Once you have duplicated the original, you can then begin to grow on the foundation to raise the bar higher. In this process, each son will have his own uniqueness that should and must be celebrated. This allows a son to stand on the father's shoulders. The duplication is the father's foundation in him and his uniqueness is built on that foundation, which raises him higher.

When you never give your sons identity, they are forced to find identity anywhere they can. We read in scripture that both the prodigal son and Joseph are given a coat as part of their identity. If fathers don't present their sons a coat, so to speak, they will find someone else's coat to wear. I can't help but make the contrast with today's society. So many of our sons are walking around wearing their favorite sports star's jersey. We wear their name on us. We look up and value who they are and we are willing to borrow their identity. While there's nothing wrong with wearing a jersey, there's something wrong when our belief in our own identity is so minimal that we need to wear another son's identity. "If only I could be like them," we say.

I'm pretty confident that I have never seen Stephen Curry wearing a Labron James Jersey. Why? Because his own identity is seen as worthy of being on his own jersey. He made the team; he is enough. He represents his name himself. What if our sons had the truth of the great identity they carry sewn into them, the last name of their Heavenly Father written on them. When we come to Christ, Holy Spirit marks us with a seal. We carry His name! We carry His identity as part of our own. Our own name is enough. We are fearfully and wonderfully made (Psalm 139:14). This is a striking statement in scripture: that God so values us that He made us with such care and concern that He would describe it as "fearfully." He had to get our creation just right.

You are made with value and it's time to know what it is that you carry. You have gold buried inside you. It's time to dig out that treasure. Let's live a life worthy of our own name on our own jersey: "Team Jesus!"

So what's in a nickname?

The Lord at times changed names but many times He simply gave a nickname. He will give you a nickname to carry identity. In Mark 3:17 Jesus gives a nickname to the disciples James and John – "Sons of Thunder." What an awesome nickname! Jesus calls Simeon "Peter," which means "Rock." So you got the original Rock, that's right; Dwayne Johnson may owe some royalties but he is not the Rock: Peter is! So there you have the three disciples that were closer to Jesus than the rest and Jesus had given them nicknames.

We learn how James and John live out this nickname when they want to call down fire on those that didn't have any manners when greeting Jesus as He arrives. Jesus rebukes them for this and tells them, "You know not what spirit you are of" (Luke 9:55). They wanted to thunder down judgment and instead Jesus teaches them to love. However, by the end of his life John, the author of the gospel of John as well as all the other books of John, focuses on Love. He turns his thunder to the love of God in his writings. Instead of calling down the fire of God as a weapon, He thunders out the heart of God, the love of God that breaks the silence of the hopelessness of sin.

"He who has an ear, let him hear what the Spirit says to the churches. To the one who conquers I will give some of the hidden manna, and I will give him a white stone, with a new name written on the stone that no one knows except the one who receives it"(Revelation 2:17).

Your earthly father gave you a first name but now it is time to let your Heavenly Father have His turn naming you. It's time for Him to breathe His life into your identity and to empower you to live out your destiny. What man calls you has no power but what God calls you can set your captive destiny free. You are more than a conqueror. You are worthy of your Father's name. The very one who spoke the stars into existence is calling out your name, your identity, your destiny. It's etched in stone and will not fade away.

Stop right now; don't read another page! You need to know who you are in God's sight. How does your Father in heaven see you? Stop and ask Him, and wait for His reply. Without the knowledge of your true identity you will always wear the identity of another.

What does God call you?

Why does He call you that?

Provider

In the natural, the idea of the provider is one who brings home the bacon; the breadwinner. He also provides protection to his family. A spiritual provider points to the ability to set up the environment for spiritual sons to have security, and to know they can become next level leaders. The provider walks with a willingness to pay the price of raising up godly sons. Trust me, raising up godly sons can cost you! It will cost you time, it will cost you prayers, and it might even cost you your reputation.

Abraham as a spiritual father is a good provider. Not only is he raising Lot, who is not his natural son, but he also is a father to Isaac. Abraham lets Lot share the resources he has and teaches him how to steward that provision. Sons have to be taught how to manage their resources. Lottery winners go broke within five years because no one taught them how to manage them. Many pastors turn the church over to staff or natural sons but never teach them how to steward the ministry, and the ministry crashes. Many businesses turn their business over to their sons who they never taught to steward the business and their business fails. Legacy dies with them usually because they should have been teaching and releasing the best to those that would succeed them.

Abraham gave Lot the choice of the best. Why? Because Abraham already knew how to grow the herd in a harsh environment, and he gave Lot a chance for the most success. Sunday school teachers, teach someone how to teach your class. Business owners, teach someone how to run your business: you might end up franchising. Franchising is the business term for being fruitful and multiplying through sons. Altar call leaders, teach people how to pray better than you. Chefs, pass on your secret recipe. Somebody under you should know what those eleven herbs and spices are.

So here's a question for all business leaders, entrepreneurs, and spiritual leaders if you're in covenant. Why are you afraid to be a good provider? Why are you walking as if resources are limited? Do you not realize that you have access to your Father's wallet, a wallet with unlimited resources? Money has no value to God, only to us. God has every resource and the word says He owns the cattle on a thousand hills (Psalm 50:10). By the way He created the hills, the grass and the cattle that He owns; if they should run out, I bet you He could go make more. Abraham is not in competition with Lot and is willing to make great sacrifices to stay in a healthy relationship with him. He allows him to grow by simply saying, "You pick what property area you want to dominate and take over. I'll take what's left and we'll both be prosperous."

Now I ask you, how many Business Leaders have tried to shut down their employees who they mentored as sons when it was seen in them that they had a desire to go and start something new. You are holding them back from developing the same character that is in you. How many church pastors have had sons rise up in their church in which God called to go start churches, and were shut down and told, "You can go do your own thing but don't you dare steal any of my people or resources!" Those pastors offer conditional blessings: "I'll bless you if you don't take from me," instead of simply following Abraham's example of walking out covenant. How many pastors are sending their sons out with a quick offering but no inheritance?

> *"Studies and anecdotal evidence indicate that if there is one church per ten thousand residents, approximately 1% of the population will be church goers. If this ratio goes to one church per one thousand residents, some 15% to 20% of the city's population goes to church. If the number goes to one per five hundred residents, the number may approach 40% or more. The relationship of the number of churches to church going people is exponential, not linear." - Tim Keller*

This means that in a town of 10,000 people, the single church in the town will have an attendance of just 100. If there are 10 churches in the same town, their attendance would be at least 150 per church. If you flood the town with 20 churches, the attendance reaches 200 per church. Competition is not a famine; it's a feast!

According to a survey conducted by the North American Mission board, only 68% of new churches planted will survive four years. I wonder if the survival rate would rise significantly if more established churches decided to parent new churches as they launch. Whatever you do will be more successful if you provision sons and duplicate it.

Consider what a healthy spiritual father might ask a son who wants to start a church, "Which people do you want to take with you, and what resources do you need to take?" Sons, we don't need you trying to leave angry and in competition either. We need sons that are Lots, not prodigals. We need ministry leaders that are Abrahams, not Sauls competing with Davids.

If you look at President Trump's family legacy, Trump's father gave him a loan to start his business and gave him the seeds of Entrepreneurship, which now Trump has clearly given to his kids. They now run a multi-billion-dollar company well because he's taught them how to steward. He gave them knowledge and opportunity and did not withhold from them the same way his father did not withhold from him. He was willing to sacrifice his horde for their success. When he got to focus on being President, that didn't stop his business from growing. That is a fatherly legacy.

Abraham's sacrifice wasn't the herd or the best land. The present land couldn't hold both the herds. By allowing Lot and his team to separate, he doubled both of their spaces for growth. Abraham could grow twice the herd. The sacrifice wasn't the sheep; it was the leader that knew how to help him shepherd. Abraham knew who his covenant provider was and he knew he could regrow the herd. He was not overcome by the famine spirit (we will discuss this punk later).

Prodigal sons waste their inheritance because they do not learn from their father's example.

Righteous fathers teach. They don't just provide fish but teach them how to fish. Righteous sons are those that mirror a righteous father. If you don't have one on earth, don't worry, you have one in heaven. We all have a righteous Father to reflect.

A true spiritual father wants those under him to surpass them. A pastor's legacy should be rooted in who he can raise up. You can grow his legacy bigger than he did.

Once a leader who is a spiritual father realizes he is in covenant with his Heavenly Father and has access to resources, he does not fear healthy competition. He begins to see value in his sons. Such value actually begins to contribute to the overall kingdom legacy. Sons in history contribute to the family's overall wealth. One of the reasons the Old Testament wanted sons is because sons could go out and work and bring resources into the family. Isn't it possible that one of the reasons God wants sons is so they can go out and work and contribute to the overall family and provide a safety net for the elderly? They can provide extra hands, extra work, extra thought processes, and new innovations. They can raise up the level of the entire family by simply contributing their gifts and their talents.

Wasn't this what Father God wanted from the very beginning? He created the heavens and the earth, then handed it over to His son and said, "Be fruitful and multiply; now let's see what you do with it" (Genesis 1:28).

Fathers provide identity, not just resources.

In King David's story we learn that Jesse failed to provide identity to David over and over again. When the prophet Samuel came to pick a king, David wasn't invited to be presented as a part of the sons of Jesse. He is painted by Jesse as something of a bastard. Even after Samuel anointed him king, Jesse sends him back to the sheep. In a time in history where kings are required to show strength through personal battle, Jesse keeps David at home and only lets him go to the battle when he is running UberEATS deliveries to his brothers. Jesse does not groom David for the role of son or a king.

In fact, it was not what Jesse gave that provided him identity. Rather it came when Samuel anointed him king and, second, when an unnamed man spoke up for David when Saul was searching for a harp player.

So Saul said to his attendants, "Find someone who plays well and bring him to me." One of the servants answered, "I have seen a son of Jesse of Bethlehem who knows how to play the lyre. He is a brave man and a warrior. He speaks well and is a fine-looking man. And the Lord is with him" (1 Samuel 16:17-18).

This unnamed man in the court of the king sees identity in David that Jesse does not see. He is called a musician, a man of valor, a warrior, an excellent preacher, and they know he carries the anointing of the Lord on his life. When they find David, he is still in the field taking care of his father's sheep. His father has failed to position David: even knowing that his son has been anointed king, he continues to position him wrongfully – as a shepherd. Right identity leads to proper positioning.

Sons, hear me out. Some of you are serving under fathers that have not seen your giftings and have failed to position you rightly. Take heart and stay faithful. David stayed faithful and submissive even in the lowly position he was placed in. If you want God to use you, then get under a father and take care of his sheep until God moves you. If you are faithful to the flock you are given, then a father will either have to reposition you or release you. David waited on God to position the anointing on his life. Some people are appointed but they are never anointed. When you allow man to position you, you will just be appointed but when you allow God to position you, you will be anointed.

Jesse finally had to release David to the king. Saul would go on to repeat the poor positioning of David. He was anointed king but was made the harpist. He rightfully won a marriage to the king's daughter when he defeated Goliath; but Saul did not provide the prize immediately. David waited faithfully much like Joseph waited faithfully. God will always position sons that honor the fathers they are under and Joseph honored his master, while David honored his king. They both faithfully served even when the fathers didn't faithfully provide what was their due. Your faithfulness will prepare your present to position your future.

Seems we have a bad dad fad. This is where fathers take anointed sons and put them out to pasture instead of allowing them to pastor. This can be a product of fear, jealousy, or lack of discernment. Some leaders fear their sons will rise up and receive such levels of favor that they will lose everything they've worked so hard to make happen. Fathers who have walked hard paths and not received help from their own fathers often think that it's only fair to make their son walk that path. They see themselves as gatekeepers instead of platform providers. Other fathers have such poor self images that they can't even see the good in their offspring.

CHAPTER 4

THE ROLES OF THE FATHER:
PROPHET, PRIEST AND KING

Prophet

An important aspect of being a prophet is that every prophet carries a mantle. In the Old Testament, the mantle was a part of the prophet's uniform and was a symbolic statement of the authority they carried. When a prophet would choose to mentor someone, that is, a son, he would go up to him and lay a mantle over him.

You might be thinking, "Currently I'm not a prophet, so how can I carry a mantle?" Well, good news; you carry the mantle of your big brother Jesus. "What mantle is that?" you ask. Ephesians chapter 1 verses 19 through 24 tells us that, when Jesus was raised from the dead, He was given the name above all names, all authority over every principality and ruler, a seat at the right hand of the Father and everything put under his feet. Therefore the mantle of Jesus is authority. In Ephesians chapter 2 verse 6 we find out that we've been raised up and seated with Him in that authority. This is the mantle you now carry as a spiritual father. Every Holy Spirit filled believer carries a mantle out of the authority of Holy Spirit.

Fathers who carry a mantle need sons so that their legacy can be doubled. Sons of this generation need a doubling anointing for the revival that's about the come. Understand that your legacy depends on whether or not you will correctly pass down your mantle. Elijah finds Elisha in a field plowing and places the mantle on him, inviting him to come and learn in the school of the prophets that he leads (1 Kings 19:19-21). Elisha follows this prophetic father and begins to emulate him and to dream of raising more prophets. As Elijah shows Elisha the power available to sons, Elijah has limits removed and begins to dream of his progeny seeing a far greater anointing.

Towards the end of Elijah's ministry when he recognizes he is about to be taken from this world, he instructs Elisha not to follow him. But Elisha knows he must because all sons follow their father's footsteps. Even when other prophets give him dire warnings, he will not be detoured. He knows there's a double anointing available to him. Elisha got his first mantle while plowing and the second while pursuing. **If you want a father's mantle then make sure you are paying the price of pursuit.**

2 Kings 2:4-11:

Elijah said to him, "Elisha, please stay here, for the Lord has sent me to Jericho." But he said, "As the Lord lives, and as you yourself live, I will not leave you." So they came to Jericho. The sons of the prophets who were at Jericho drew near to Elisha and said to him, "Do you know that today the Lord will take away your master from over you?" And he answered, "Yes, I know it; keep quiet."

Then Elijah said to him, "Please stay here, for the Lord has sent me to the Jordan." But he said, "As the Lord lives, and as you

*yourself live, I will not leave you." So the two of them went on.
Fifty men of the sons of the prophets also went and stood at some
distance from them, as they both were standing by the Jordan.
Then Elijah took his cloak and rolled it up and struck the water,
and the water was parted to the one side and to the other, till the
two of them could go over on dry ground.*

*When they had crossed, Elijah said to Elisha, "Ask what I shall
do for you, before I am taken from you." And Elisha said, "Please
let there be a double portion of your spirit on me." And he said,
"You have asked a hard thing; yet, if you see me as I am being
taken from you, it shall be so for you, but if you do not see me,
it shall not be so." And as they still went on and talked, behold,
chariots of fire and horses of fire separated the two of them. And
Elijah went up by a whirlwind into heaven.*

A spiritual father chooses his words wisely because he understands
that he can either complain and speak death over his sons, or he
can come into agreement with heaven and begin to speak to the
destiny that was put upon them from their mother's womb. This
is why the role of prophet is such an important role in a spiritual
father. In the Old Testament, prophet Samuel walked out his
spiritual responsibility of prophet by anointing two different sons.
In both situations he was speaking destiny over their lives. One of
the deepest longings in the hearts of every son is for their father
to cast vision over them and to speak of their desire for their son
to have an incredible future.

1 Samuel 3:3-9

*The lamp of God had not yet gone out, and **Samuel was lying
down in the temple of the Lord**, where the ark of God was.
Then the Lord called Samuel, and he said, "Here I am!" and ran*

to Eli and said, "Here I am, for you called me." But he said, "I did not call; lie down again." So he went and lay down. And the Lord called again, "Samuel!" and Samuel arose and went to Eli and said, "Here I am, for you called me." But he said, "I did not call you my son; lie down again."

Now Samuel did not yet know the Lord, and the word of the Lord had not yet been revealed to him. And the Lord called Samuel again the third time. And he arose and went to Eli and said, "Here I am, for you called me." Then Eli perceived that the Lord was calling the boy. Therefore Eli said to Samuel, "Go, lie down, and if he calls you, you shall say, 'Speak, Lord, for your servant hears.'" So Samuel went and lay down in his place" (emphasis added).

Fathers who operate as prophets will also raise up prophets and teach their sons how to hear the voice of God.

While Eli may not have been a good father to his sons, he was a good father to Samuel in that he taught him how to hear and respond to the voice of the Lord. It's interesting that the Scriptures make reference to the fact that Eli's vision had gone dim. The nation of Israel was turning pagan because fathers were not operating as prophets and priests. When you don't operate as prophets and priests, you become dim to the voice of the Lord and you allow sin and mixture in the house. Eli will later become completely blind but right now he has enough spiritual clarity to recognize when the young son Samuel is hearing from the Lord. Wow! Even though one is going dim, there is still a fire burning in the tabernacle.

Fathers will position their sons to hear God.

Another interesting point behind what is mentioned in the scriptures is that Eli was sleeping in his usual place but Eli the father has positioned his son to be in a place where he could hear from the Lord. Note where Samuel is sleeping. Samuel is sleeping near the ark of the covenant. If you want to become prophetic, you rest to get into the presence of the Lord. And, even though the nation of Israel rarely heard the prophetic words uttered, there was still hope because the lamp of the Lord was still burning. The lamp of the Lord refers to the menorah, which I believe is a type and shadow of Holy Spirit.

Eli knew the power of a son learning to listen to the father's voice, even if it meant being woken up in the middle of the night. A good father also doesn't underestimate his son's ability to hear from God just because of his age or maturity, although he may need help to process what the Lord is saying. Remember the words of Eli next time you hear the word of the Lord; say, "Your servant is listening."

As a father your voice should echo the voice of God so much so your sons are unable to tell the difference. Without careful and purposeful intimacy, you'll miss your transformation into the image of our Heavenly Father. The goal in our devotion should be to become so intimate with Father God that those around us can hardly tell where God ends and we begin.

Samuel was a true spiritual father, prophet, and priest. He was also a king maker. Fathers with a prophetic authority can produce kings. Samuel raised up sons higher than himself. Pastors, leaders, if you are not raising the next man up, someone that doesn't just take your place but rise higher than you, then you need to take a lesson from Samuel. **There are churches today that are one heart attack away from closing their doors and seeing legacy leave. We have pastors and leaders that are producing good fruit but have never produced another plant.** When a fruit tree with good fruit is finally uprooted and it has not produced other fruit trees, it's called extinction. Ask yourself this question now: if today is your day to leave your work undone, is there someone you have raised up that will carry on what you began?

Ren recently asked a question to a room full of senior pastors. "If you died today who would carry on your call of ministry; who is your Elisha?" He was not at all shocked by the replies.

Several echoed the same thing. "Well that's not a problem in my denomination; they just assign someone new to the church." This is the fundamental problem. We have ministers that somehow believe that the building is your ministry.

Your call of ministry is your heart, your spiritual DNA, and your anointing. It's unique to you. Elijah trained up Elisha to not only walk in that anointing but to double it. He carried on the heart of Elijah's ministry. A pastor can be replaced but the new one, if he has not embraced the heart, will function in a totally different way from his predecessor. The former pastor may have a heart for the homeless or the struggling, while the new pastor has the heart for teaching and raising leaders. Both are good but, just because the church has the same name and the same people, does not mean your calling is perpetuated. How many ministries have died because the figure leading it died? They had powerful ministries but never raised up sons to carry and steward the father's anointing as Elijah did with Elisha.

If you have become a spiritual father, the legacy of your anointing will continue. Anointed men and women have great stories in history books but anointed spiritual fathers are still changing lives through anointings passed on.

Raising up leaders is not always easy. Sometimes, like Samuel, we make corrections but, if our sons are Sauls, they reject correction. Samuel shows us how a true spiritual father reacts in his heart.

The Lord said to Samuel, "How long will you grieve over Saul, since I have rejected him from being king over Israel? Fill your horn with oil, and go. I will send you to Jesse the Bethlehemite, for I have provided for myself a king among his sons" (1 Samuel 16:1).

A true father mourns the failures of a son. When leaders' disciples fail, it should break our hearts; it should not stir us to anger. Samuel mourned and his heart was heavy. Too many pastors just care for sheep because you grieve less over the loss of a sheep than you do a son. Sheep are easier to guide because they just want to be led to green pastures, whereas sons want to own the green pastures. A true father recognizes that a son is, first, a son of God before he is a son of man. Saul was God's to deal with before he was Samuel's.

Priest

The role of priest is one of ecclesiastical ordination. In the Old Testament a Levitical Priest like Eli would educate, bless, perform sacrifices and exercise judgment of Torah. How does this apply to today's spiritual fathers? Just like natural fathers, spiritual fathers are charged with bringing up their sons in the ways of the Lord. The role of the priest is an opportunity to speak blessings over your spiritual sons as in the role of prophet: what you forth tell matters. Therefore speaking blessings will serve as an encouragement and even a healing balm against all of the words spoken against your spiritual sons.

The LORD bless you and keep you; the LORD make his face to shine upon you and be gracious to you; the LORD lift up his countenance upon you and give you peace (Numbers 6:24-26).

As priests, we no longer offer animal sacrifices but we do have the opportunity to teach our spiritual sons how to offer up the sacrifice of praise. Here we send up our worship to thank God for His goodness and blessings. Spiritual fathers get the sacred opportunity to go to God on behalf of our sons.

The role of teaching and judging the Torah to our spiritual sons matters because we cannot sit by idly and allow our kids to do anything they choose. **Eli gave instruction without correction. Instruction is self help; correction brings repentance.** Silent fathers that don't correct will raise up murderous sons as we clearly see in David's failures with his four sons, Adonijah, Amnon, Absalom, and even Solomon. When a father tries to step in and finally correct murderous sons, it will lead to sons murdering the father. We will expand on Eli's murderous sons in a later chapter.

We have watched as pastors and leaders have waited so long to bring correction to those they are charged with that, when they do, those individuals in positions of leadership begin to manifest the murderous intent stirring in them. They don't leave the church or workplace quietly but poison the well as they leave. They try to destroy the church. Their excuse is that this church is a fraud and they truly believe they are doing a service by forcing the church to lose members or hurting the business clients so that they will see its demise. Without correction, the sons will create belief systems and justify them, saying that their actions were acceptable to God. They think they are helping God out and can't see that their actions are, in fact, the definition of witchcraft by the word.

1 Samuel 3:11-14:

Then the Lord said to Samuel, "Behold, I am about to do a thing in Israel at which the two ears of everyone who hears it will tingle. On that day I will fulfill against Eli all that I have spoken concerning his house, from beginning to end. And I declare to him that I am about to punish his house forever, for the iniquity that he knew, because his sons were blaspheming God, and he did not restrain them. Therefore I swear to the house of Eli that the iniquity of Eli's house shall not be atoned for by sacrifice or offering forever."

One of the judgments upon Eli was that he would have his generations cut off forever. Both of his sons would die on the same day. One of the worst abuses of a spiritual father to his sons, is simply neglect. Neglect is a particularly ominous foe. It is probably one of the hardest to treat because it can be hard to find. When a person experiences a traumatic event, they have something concrete to point to as the root of wounding. But with neglect it's not that easy. It is difficult to know that neglect is a traumatic root because it's a lack of something, not an addition of something. So the neglected many times do not know they have been in lack. They don't know what they should have had.

Jesse is guilty of constantly neglecting David, treating him as an illegitimate son. Most bible scholars believe David was in fact an illegitimate son, born of a sinful relationship and not of Jesse's wife. Whatever the reason, Jesse neglects David. This is one of the reasons David is most likely one of the most traumatized biblical characters.

With Eli, his neglect was one where he simply never corrected his children's wrongdoing. To neglect correction leaves a void that will be filled by a son's misdirected thoughts. As leaders, we are charged by God with the vision of the house. A father's neglect means the leader is never sharing and releasing vision over his sons. What are the consequences of Eli's neglect? That a spiritual son was forced to give correction to a father. It was a godly role reversal. This answers our question in the beginning. Eli's generation was cut off because of his lack of correction and neglect regarding their abusive conduct. Samuel rises up to be a godly spiritual father, who unabashedly gives correction to king Saul. When Saul refuses correction, Samuel raises up David. He fears no spiritual son, not even a king, because he saw the outcome of Eli's passivity.

Our pastors need to cry out for sons, not seats filled. In the Introduction we asked the question why would God use two fatherless sons to write a book about fathers. Hannah shows us the answer. She is this generation's prayer for revival. She is at the doorpost crying out, "Give me a legacy!" And Eli the gatekeeper, the sonless father, the father who was incapable of raising up sons, was judging Hannah saying, "Oh foolish woman; how long will you be drunk?" But Hannah's cry is not to fill seats in church, or be recognized amongst the peers. She didn't say, "Give me a huge congregation, or grow my ministry!" She was crying, "Give me a son!"

We have a fatherless generation whose fathers have not produced sons. God is saying: "I'll answer the cry of the Hannahs and give them a Samuel and I'll raise up a son who will become a father to the nation. Eli could not raise up sons but Samuel raises up spiritual sons. He raises up Saul and rebukes him. God used Samuel because Samuel would even give correction to sons that were kings. Then Samuel raises up a David through whom the lineage of Jesus comes because he could correct and nurture that relationship.

King

Samuel is a prophet but he is also a king maker. He is the most powerful man in Israel but the people want a king. Instead of continuing to hold on to his unshared power, Samuel raises up and anoints Saul king. After Saul's failure Samuel sets out to find a new king for Israel and that's when Samuel is led to the house of Jesse.

As fathers, we give names, we provide, we are prophets and priests. But we are also kings. We provide inheritance and legacy.

We have heard how David is overlooked over and over again. Yet, somehow, David models loyalty and honor through his mighty men. Just the name alone shows you how David refused to repeat the pattern of neglect of his father. David is a man who honors his men. We never read anywhere in the word that any of David's men ever betray him. Even the enemy kings open their arms to David. Almost everyone is loyal to David, except his fathers, Jesse and Saul.

Bringing correction

David and Ren are a lot alike. Ren's father was neglectful for the most part; but Ren has done his best to refuse that image and to focus on his role as a father. Really, the only pattern we see repeated in David's life is that of Samuel. However, David is slow to bring correction to his biological sons. One of them Absalom tries to usurp the throne from David himself and the other Adonijah tries to usurp the throne from Solomon (2 Samuel 18; 1 King 1:5-8). What made his son Adonijah think he could do such a thing?

> *His father had never at any time displeased him by asking, "Why have you done thus and so?* (1 Kings 1:6a)

In fact, David had never brought correction to his sons. He resuscitates the same pattern from Eli that should have been corrected. Three generations are plagued with sons that have never been corrected. You can tell this is more than likely a learned behavior of David's because it is actually very out of character for him in his personal belief system. David is a man after God's own heart who was open to correction and quick to repent in his own life. He trusted God and took His rebukes. So we can see this pattern on Eli has flowed down to the sons of David. What broken patterns did your fathers carry that you are allowing to flow down to the next generation under you?

To neglect your sons by withholding love, position, or correction will always leave them vulnerable to destruction. This is especially dangerous when you are dealing with kings. Wounded and damaged leaders are in a position to damage much more than themselves. It's so important the church begins to raise up kings again. As the prophet anoints kings, so must the leaders of the church be the spiritual fathers who raise up and correct kings once more. Most of the church has somehow forgotten that we are kingmakers. We have resigned ourselves to simply raising up priests. It's amazing in this politically charged environment how many Christian leaders we see foaming and railing over the godless government we have. But most of the church has relinquished raising up men and women in godly governance subduing godless institutions, and we are reaping what our social order has sown. When the fatherly priests once again accept their authority and commission of raising up righteous representatives in our government, then will we see a shift in politics. We are the kings and the kingmakers. We need to declare godly leaders over our nations again.

For our leaders, what we speak over our sons has the power to shape them. When kings speak, it becomes law forever. The decree of a king is permanent. Start speaking life over those you are ruling over. Make them heirs, not subjects. Your Father in heaven has done the same for you. He has made you a joint heir of the promise (Romans 8:17). We must recognize the authority we carry and impart it to those we are raising up.

Influence without authority makes you simply a friend. Authority without influence makes you a dictator. But the one who walks in both authority and influence walks as a king.

Only a person *with* authority can *give* authority. If you don't believe that, try this fun little experiment: ask one of your coworkers for the day off instead of your boss. A spiritual father has the authority as king to place a spiritual son in the position of kingship! In the Old Testament, fathers would give their oldest born son a birthright which placed them as head over the household. Kingdoms fall due to the rise of illegitimate kings.

So many members in the church think they have a right to rule over fathers. If the pastor doesn't do it their way, they are angry and leave or slander him. You cannot claim authority: it must be given. We cannot tell you how many people have tried to dictate the direction of the church when in their own lives, their children, marriages and friendships are all filled with dysfunction. When the results of your advice first produce good fruit in your family, then as pastors we can allow your counsel to bear fruit in the spiritual family of the church. Fathers, our role is to give and protect authority.

Our society has an aversion to the role of father as king. This might be because many associate kingship and authority with oppression and abuse. God sets up spiritual authority and says Jesus is King of Kings. The Bible even tells us that Jesus was given all authority, and a name above every name. At the name of Jesus everything will bow. Jesus is sat at the right hand of the Father and everything is under His feet (Ephesians 1:19-24). The amazing thing is that we who place our trust in Jesus are raised up to sit with King Jesus (Ephesians 2:4-6). Jesus is called King of Kings because we are Kings and He is King over us! So we now know that we have authority because we are given authority from someone with Authority. When we can place ourselves underneath Jesus, He gives us authority.

Often to gain authority, you have to place yourself under people. In Matthew chapter 8, we read of a centurion who walks in high levels of faith simply because he understands how authority works!

> *When he had entered Capernaum, a centurion came forward to him, appealing to him, "Lord, my servant is lying paralyzed at home, suffering terribly." And he said to him, "I will come and heal him." But the centurion replied, "Lord, I am not worthy to have you come under my roof, but only say the word, and my servant will be healed. For I too am a man under authority, with soldiers under me. And I say to one, 'Go,' and he goes, and to another, 'Come,' and he comes, and to my servant, 'Do this,' and he does it." When Jesus heard this, he marveled and said to those who followed him, "Truly, I tell you, with no one in Israel have I found such faith. I tell you, many will come from east and west and recline at table with Abraham, Isaac, and Jacob in the kingdom of heaven, while the sons of the kingdom will be thrown into the outer darkness. In that place there will be weeping and gnashing of teeth." And to the centurion Jesus said, "Go; let it be done for you as you have believed." And the servant was healed at that very moment (Matthew 8:5-13).*

The centurion is not Jewish and has no religious background but he sees the authority Jesus has. His statement about being unworthy points to his recognition of the holiness of Jesus and his next statement points to his understanding of Jesus' authority: "Say the word and my servant will be healed." Jesus carries all authority and at His command the armies of Heaven will be dispatched to accomplish His desire. The bible says that Jesus marveled at the centurion, in other words, He was filled with wonder, admiration, or astonishment. Think about that! This man's request and understanding of authority caused even Jesus, the Son of God, to be filled with such amazement. Jesus shares with those around Him that He hasn't seen faith like this in all of Israel. Then Jesus makes another powerful statement that almost seems out of place to the modern reader.

> "I tell you, many will come from east and west and recline at table with Abraham, Isaac, and Jacob in the kingdom of heaven, while the sons of the kingdom will be thrown into the outer darkness. In that place there will be weeping and gnashing of teeth" (Matthew 8:11-12).

I believe this passage is crucial in understanding the power of correct godly authority and the need for spiritual fathers walking in that authority. Jesus is warning us that religious practices without submission to God's Authority may give us a sense of security but that is a false security and will ultimately engulf us in greater darkness.

We now have a generation of churches who have no spiritual father and the crazy thing about that lack is that it means that they have no true place to gain or grow in authority. Authority comes from our Father, but then it is delegated to spiritual fathers who become the fields where spiritual sons can sow the seeds of loyalty and honor, and reap the harvest of greater authority. Currently, you have churches running around without any sense of authority, which means they walk in no power. This lack has also created people who are walking in false Authority.

Kings versus Peasants

In order to be successful leaders, we need to begin to see ourselves differently. We need the filter of identity through heaven's gaze. You are a kingdom citizen but not just any citizen. You are royalty! You are the heirs not peasants. If you want to walk out that identity then you need to understand the mindset of a king versus a peasant.

You need to become kingdom minded, like kings. Kings are focused on the whole kingdom and its people. Peasants are focused on their family and small circle. A peasant is not particularly interested in the blight of the next town or even possibly his neighbor's. A peasant is concerned with his house, the size, quality, land, crops etc. His ability to provide for his own is a central theme.

A king, on the other hand, is not concerned with just his palace. He is thinking about infrastructure, roads, bridges, food supplies, farmers, schools, business development, trade etc. A kingdom minded man knows his job is to build the kingdom not just his palace. In America, we have never judged the success of a president based on whether he expanded the size of the Whitehouse. We ask if he expanded the stock market, travel, trade, prosperity to the people and if people feel their lives were better because he served the people. A king serves those he calls subjects; a peasant serves those he calls master.

When an invading army descends or a plague ravages the land, a peasant will hide in hopes of riding out the disaster upon his house. His primary concern is his home and those in his circle. A king, to the contrary, begins to move and order those at his command to fight. He orders doctors and brings in supplies. A kingdom minded man does not just care for his own but is concerned about the welfare of others.

In ministry you can see this. Kings build kingdoms, not homes. The kingdom, ministry, or business that God has given you is always bigger than yourself. It takes many hands helping to see a kingdom built. If you can accomplish the call of God on your life alone, then it is probably not God's call. He always wants you to partner with others. If you are focused only on the ministry God gave you, then you have the peasant mentality. As kingdom builders we should be looking for help with our call and looking at who we can help in theirs. We should be coming alongside other kingdom citizens to see them rise up and live out their unique calling. Only then are we kings building kingdoms.

If you only care about what you get out of church, you might be a peasant. A peasant is a hireling, never the boss. The king, or owner, sees all the areas that need growth and monitoring. He sees that the copy machine is down, that the coffee pot is empty. He pays attention to the function of the organization as a whole. A peasant, an employee, just sees their own cubicle. A peasant mentality is not aware of how their actions affect those around them. Ren has visited churches before where the front was full of flag wavers. As he stood on the front row; the flag wavers were enjoying themselves as they waved away. Ren however was not. He was in a training session of dip, duck, dodge, and dive. The flag wavers were totally unaware as they were hitting him with their flags. It was a huge distraction to him in his attempt to worship. A peasant mentality is not aware or simply doesn't process how their needs or actions impact others. Kings cultivate all of the kingdom. Before you decide to be annoyed at rules, ask yourself, is this rule here to protect people from the mindless actions of others?

Inviting in Jezebel

One of the worst consequences of not walking in correct authority is that it opens the door to the spirit of Jezebel. Jezebel was an Old Testament queen who had no power except that King Ahab surrendered his authority to her. Jezebel usurped Ahab's power and entrenched Israel in Baal worship and gross sexual immorality. The reason Jezebel is running rampant in our country right now is because there are no spiritual fathers walking in Authority. There is no King to say "You will stop!" Therefore she continues to usurp power and, before long, the spirit of Jezebel is overtaking a place.

The Jezebel spirit has twin children – famine and poverty. These evil children help Jezebel lock generations into endless cycles of strongholds. When there are no spiritual fathers operating as kings, there is no one telling Jezebel, "You have no authority here and you must bow your knee to the name of Jesus!" Spiritual fathers can break the stronghold and restore correct authority to the body of Christ. It starts with leaders who will submit to Jesus.

We need to be careful to wield authority, not as a weapon but as a tool to serve the body of Christ. King Jesus fights religion but also washes the feet of His disciples. A king must stand firm on God's word but must also walk out a servant lifestyle and serve those under their authority. Can you honestly say that you serve your spiritual sons? Or are you a dictator to your servants?

CHAPTER 5

THE TWIN SPIRITS

"A poor mouth is the first to lower its standards
in times of famine."
~Ren Schuffman

We are going to talk about a spiritual mindset/spirit called famine and poverty, This demonic assignment aids, abets and contributes to the bastard spirit. These two spirits may look like twins but they have different fingerprints. While they have a lot of similar effects on people, their motivation is different.

First, we need to make clear that all mindsets, both godly and demonic, good and bad, start out first as thoughts. Thoughts form a belief, then an action, then a habit that cultivates a culture, and, finally, they invade your spirit and take control. What these mindsets are depends on the belief system you form and stand by. Understand that everything in the natural is mirrored in the supernatural. The biological effects of famine are a reflection of the spiritual effects on the soul.

Let's dive into these two spiritual mindsets, famine and poverty, and see how they gain ground on us.

The Famine Spirit

The famine spirit and mindset can affect individuals, families, communities, organizations, and even control nations. While natural famine is brought on by the lack of food and resources, spiritual famine comes from a lack of encounters with God and His word.

> *"Behold, the days are coming," declares the Lord God, "when I will send a famine on the land—not a famine of bread, nor a thirst for water, but of hearing the words of the Lord. They shall wander from sea to sea, and from north to east; they shall run to and fro, to seek the word of the Lord, but they shall not find it"* (Amos 8:11-12).

Causes of Famine

True spiritual famine comes from not hearing God's voice. This spirit can be brought on by a casual attitude towards the things that displease God and a continual acceptance of sin. Let's look at Eli again. When we discussed the idea that fathers are the spiritual priests, you would have noticed that at the time when Samuel was raised up by Eli, who was in a spiritual slumber, the scriptures say that visions and revelations from the Lord were rare. Why was this so? Because there was an acceptance of sin in the camp and mixture in the tabernacle.

When spiritual fathers fail to correct their sons, it causes a void which sin begins to fill. One of the things we want to always watch as followers of Christ is that our hearts are always sensitive to the convicting of sin by Holy Spirit. We want to live a life in which we are constantly seeking holiness and being in the presence of God.

One of the causes of famine in the natural is crop failure. In the natural, continual failures will lead to an expectancy that you will continue to be without. In the spiritual, it starts with continual spiritual dryness, which leads you into the mindset that you're going to experience spiritual lack. Because you are losing your connection with God, your spiritual senses are dulled, your direction is unclear, and your vision is blur. A blurred vision leads to the death of destiny and the draining of any hope of walking in God's plan. Hosea 4:6 says, "*My people are destroyed for lack of knowledge…*"

War is another cause of natural famine. The longer a war is prolonged, the more the risk of a famine, for resources will go towards the war effort rather than food production. For a family who has lived in a long season of spiritual warfare, it's easy to step into a famine mindset. Famine caused by natural and spiritual warfare leads you to focus so heavily on fighting for survival that you no longer realize your own hunger signals are out of balance. Your need to feed is suppressed and soon your body begins to display signs of malnutrition, disease and dysfunction. With spiritual famine, the enemy keeps you so busy fighting fires started by him that you never have time to look after your own spiritual health. You have no time to grow and feed your soul. When you stop receiving the bread of life, you become spiritually malnourished. You are so exhausted from continual battling that you don't have any energy to eat a proper meal, or to prepare the bread of life, which develops spiritual strength and fortitude. But you are not called to be a firefighter putting out all the enemy's fires; you're called to be a fire starter to cook a hearty meal and to warm your soul.

But God's goodness can always turn things around. He promises from His word that, even in war, He will make your enemies *bread* for you, for He will go before you. That's the decree Caleb made about the enemies in the Promised Land:

*"And do not fear the people of the land, **for they are bread for us**. Their protection is removed from them..."* (Numbers 14:9, emphasis added).

The above scripture shows that a father who operates in the promises of God will even receive provision from his enemies. Recounting how God caused the children of Israel to take city after city, Joshua relates how their provision had indeed come from their enemies,

> *"I gave you a land on which you had not labored and cities that you had not built, and you dwell in them. You eat the fruit of vineyards and olive orchards that you did not plant"* (Joshua 24:13).

Another factor that leads to famine in communities is a track record of malnutrition that goes back for generations. The community or nation have a long-standing history of not knowing how to properly feed their population, either through poor agricultural practices, poor distribution of food, or corruption. In a spiritual famine, your history may point to a generational curse of spiritual malnutrition.

Let me give you an example. A church that has been constantly feeding its people on a diet of the prosperity gospel and little else is in danger of bringing up children who are fat and flabby with no muscle. It's like feeding your child cake and ice cream and little else. Not that teaching prosperity is bad, but neglecting to teach the whole counsel of God, including the need for repentance and sacrifice, leaves the congregation weak and unable to stand when adversity strikes. And it will!

Again, when sons don't chase after their Heavenly Father, they will squander the Father's gifts and find themselves in the midst of famine. God loves you so much that He will not force you to be in relationship with Him. Neither will He force you to serve Him or even be His son. God has given you a free will and wants you into exercise it responsibly. This is the picture we see in the prodigal son parable, which bears repeating because there is so much revelation here. The father allowed his son to exercise his free will at a high price: he sold his land and freely gave his son his inheritance even after the son basically says, "I wish you were dead because, if you were dead, I would get my inheritance and the freedom to do what I want." Look at it this way: the son has access to everything the father has but he does not value it.

We see the same behavior played out in people who have a poverty mindset. Go to an impoverished city where the government provides for the needs of the people. How do the people of that city treat the city? How do they treat the houses that they don't pay for? How do they treat the clothing and the food they don't have to work for? When you have an impoverished mindset, you can have access to resources but you will not value or correctly utilize those resources. Like the prodigal son, such people have access to everything the city provides; yet they are ungrateful.

So, even though the father knows that the prodigal son operates under a poverty spirit, he gives him his inheritance and freedom prematurely. The father knows his son will squander his property. When you walk in a poverty mindset and use your own will as license to do whatever your heart desires, you will waste your gifts. When you walk away from your Father and from His will, you will always find yourself in famine.

We are living in a generation that is plagued by a spiritual famine, not a famine of food or water but a lack of encounter with the Father and the word (Amos 8:11). When you walk away from the Father, who is there to correct you? Some of us do not realize that, even though God is a good Father, He is ultimately our Master. He provides for us and takes care of us; but He also desires to direct our path. And, because He is directing our path, we feel we're being told what we can't do. So we try to run away from God to get our freedom and then end up serving a master who doesn't provide for us. The next thing we know we're surrounded in pig filth.

Consequences of Famine

We would like to give you some severe warnings about famine. Did you know that prolonged famine can lead to cannibalism? We see this in the days where Nebuchadnezzar besieged Jerusalem in 588 B.C. (2 Kings 6:24-33) where we have accounts of mothers eating their own babies. By the same token, how many Christians and ministries have begun to eat their own people because they believe there is not enough to go round and someone else might take it from you? They feel, for the sake of survival, that it's better to consume their resources and people than be consumed by them.

Yet another natural consequence of famine is severe disruption of communication. In the natural realm, when nations and communities fail to communicate logistical plans regarding supplies, confusion abounds and, where confusion is released, fear is not far behind. People can panic out of fear of lack and may commit desperate acts to save themselves We have only to see the effects of the Covid-19 lockdowns in some cities where "civilized" people started fighting over goods in the supermarkets for fear of shortages.

A similar famine mentality can come upon the children of fathers who refuse to communicate or just do not communicate well enough that there is enough. The famine mentality will cause the children to imagine all kinds of scenarios to justify immoral acts such as stealing and drug pushing in order to feed themselves. In the last analysis, what feeds you will sustain you; what you are hungry for will determine who you serve. Do you hunger and thirst after the things of God or will you serve the world system that leads to your impoverishment? The world's provision will soon leave you starving, but Jesus gives living bread and living water so satisfying that you will never hunger or thirst again: *"I am the bread of life; whoever comes to me shall not hunger, and whoever believes in me shall never thirst"* (John 5:35).

The famine mindset says your enemies will always come and take away your supply. But God's word tells us in Psalm 23:5 that He prepares a table for you even in the presence of your enemies. God is your supply and your enemy has no access to that which the Lord provided. If the enemy can take it, then it didn't come from God. No son can take away your ministry or business if it comes from God. As pastors, both of us have had people not only leave but convince others to leave our churches. If those people left because they were able to be stolen, then they did not come from His table or they were meant to be feasting at some other pastor's table. And so, we blessed them.

Another consequence of the famine spirit is the cultural pattern that evolves. Fathers keep on teaching their sons what they themselves learned from their elders and that is how to survive in a famine-conscious environment instead of rising out of it and breaking the cycle. Families who are dominated by famine spirit will always produce children who are at high risk of repeating this as a generational curse. They exhibit symptoms of miserliness both in the natural and spiritual by holding back giving within the family and to others. They become oblivious of God's clear command to increase and multiply.

Famine in the natural environment also affects pregnant women who, owing to malnutrition, will produce stillborn and low birth weight babies. Similarly, leaders who have the famine mentality will not produce strong and healthy disciples. Their offspring may not survive the birthing process where strength is required. Or they will come out weak. Interns, managers, new pastors, ministry volunteers, church planters with a famine mentality will grow up sickly, highly dependent on the pastor to initiate growth, and lacking in confidence to step out.

Another noticeable mental effect of the famine spirit is the tendency to hoard. This, in turn, will cause cycles of scarcity and rising prices. It will also breed a gypsy mentality of moving from place to place in search of better resources, and so people never put down roots. Some believers are called to go to other ministries that better equip them for their calling. But many may hop from church to church because they fear they are missing food they cannot get where they are, believing they can be better fed at the next church. The cycle never stops and they never dig in. The heartbreak of this is that we as Christians never learn to be a part of a community and so we stay isolated. All predators, both natural and spiritual, are always on the look out for those in isolation to attack and devour, for they are easy prey, as we see when the Amalekites attacked those who ventured out of their camp without approval in Numbers 14:44-45.

Sons, be very careful when you want to be released from being under leadership. You open yourself to danger when you leave prematurely. Many times we are desperate to be used at higher levels and want our kingdom inheritance now before we have learned to steward it. In other words, if you leave a good shepherd before you're released by God, you may find yourself with a bad master surrounded by greedy pigs. This bad master does not care what the prodigal does as long as the swine are fed. He doesn't care that the prodigal is starving. The famine spirit will enslave its victims to masters pretending to be good shepherds. Beware because they are really wolves. **When you won't serve a father who feeds you, you will end up serving a master who doesn't care if you starve.**

Breaking the famine spirit

So the question which arises is how to break the famine spirit? The answer starts with how you eat. I was asking myself the question after hearing a radio commercial about storing food for times of crisis. The product the commercial was selling was stored food that could stay in your garage for up to 25 years. Naturally, that would make great sense, so I started praying and asking the Lord why we can't store spiritual food like natural food. The answer is manna.

When you read about the Lord's provision for the children of Israel in the desert on their way to the Promised Land, it was manna. The instructions were to take exactly what they needed for the day, nothing more. If they were to take more mana than they needed (except the day before the Sabbath), it would be rotten by the next morning. Ultimately, our manna represents the freshness of our experience with Jesus and the word. This spiritual food must be received daily in order to stay fresh. So how do you break the famine spirit? You start by feeding yourself with daily spiritual food from the bread of life! What about the manna already stored in our mind and in our spirit? Yes, that testifies to the goodness and faithfulness of God and it builds on our faith to believe in His promises. But, essentially, the word has to be new every morning because of the need for fresh revelation: "*The steadfast love of the Lord never ceases; his mercies never come to an end; they are new every morning; great is your faithfulness*" (Lamentations 3:22-23).

But beware of the provision of the enemy disguising itself as good.

Because famine is a crisis of lack, the enemy will try to buy you out, but what they are selling is your future slavery, the slavery of rebellion, addiction, and people-dependence. They are selling temporary satisfaction but have now acquired your inheritance and giftings.

Remember Joseph's role as administrator during the famine in Egypt? Pharoah's rescue package seemed like a good deal – but was it so benevolent? Pharaoh buys out all the land of those who fall victim of the famine and eventually enslaves them by exacting a 20 percent levy on all they produce on their former land that now belongs to him:

> So Joseph bought all the land of Egypt for Pharaoh, for all the Egyptians sold their fields, because the famine was severe on them. The land became Pharaoh's. As for the people, he made servants of them from one end of Egypt to the other...Then Joseph said to the people, "Behold, I have this day **bought you and your land for Pharaoh**. Now here is seed for you, and you shall sow the land. And at the harvests you shall **give a fifth to Pharaoh**, and four fifths shall be your own, as seed for the field and as food for yourselves and your households, and as food for your little ones" (Genesis 47:20-21;23-25, emphasis added).

The bible tells us that "the borrower is slave to the lender" (Proverbs 22:7). In other words, your life is controlled by the person you look to for provision. Good fathers make sons; bad fathers make slaves.

Even when you find yourself surrounded by famine and a master who doesn't care if you live or die, there's still hope. You can run back to the Father. You have a loving Father who wants to bring you out of sin, bring you out of the pig filth and out of bondage. When you come back to your senses, it is time to repent. So we see the prodigal son finally going back to his father and asking for forgiveness. The father receives his prodigal son back and, even though the prodigal son has been wallowing in the pigsty, the father does something unusual. He embraces him.

Perhaps I can explain how unusual it is by sharing about a time that pastor Terry brought a baby pig to church. The pig was supposed to be a visual learning tool to help those he was teaching remember the prodigal story. But within five minutes of letting the pig loose in the church, the entire place stank. The smell was so terrible that every door and window had to be opened and everyone's eyes were watering. Anyone who's ever gone into a pig pen knows that you cannot bring the boots you wear in the pen into the house because they will stink forever. So when the prodigal son is being hugged and kissed by his father, think of the smell of the pigsty on him which the father just ignores, overpowering as it is.

That's the Father's love embracing us in spite of the stench of sin on us. It's that love that causes us to repent, for "*the goodness of God leads you to repentance*" (Romans 2:4 NKJV). Not only does the Father love us, He forgives us and covers us with His finest robe. A lot of the time we are not receiving the Father's forgiveness and strive to make ourselves clean and worthy through our own efforts; but it's the robe wrapped around you that makes you righteous. This means that spiritual fathers have the opportunity to bring their sons out of famine and transgression by offering them forgiveness and putting them back into right standing with God and them.

Spiritual fathers also have the opportunity to restore identity to their sons. The prodigal son has rehearsed a speech saying,

"I'm not worthy to be your son, let me be your slave and servant." But even before he can finish that statement, the father is already calling out to the servants to bring the best robe. Repentance is always the response to an encounter with the Lord. Anyone that does not repent rarely hears His voice.

So the key to breaking famine is running back to the Father and living a repentant lifestyle. And the way to stay out of the famine spirit is to eat properly everyday. Are you eating your daily bread? The idea of storing up food to prevent famine only works in the natural but not in the spiritual.

The Poverty Spirit
When wealth doesn't serve you and you serve wealth, that's a poverty mentality. That becomes your new master. The poverty mindset manifests itself in discontentment, greed and wrong thinking. It is motivated by greed, laziness, injustice but it can also due to lack of fathers. Someone who has a poverty mindset views their possessions as promoting self value but never understands the value of those possessions. To them, money is a number but doesn't hold actual value as a tool. A car is a symbol of status, not a tool for quickly arriving at your destination.

When you hold a poverty mentality, you begrudge people their right to success. You believe that profit, achievement and even productivity are sinful and carnal rather than the virtuous attributes that God meant them to be. It's easy to view things from a victim standpoint saying, "They don't understand what I've been through," while looking at someone who is productive and judging them to be carnal and greedy. Ultimately, nurturing a poverty mindset will darken your outlook, it will erase your dreams, it will delay your plans, kill your motivations and eventually destroy your future.

A little sleep, a little slumber, a little folding of the hands to rest, and poverty will come upon you like a robber, and want like an armed man (Proverbs 24:33-34).

In fact, since physical and spiritual poverty are closely allied, experiencing a lack of a father, or fatherlessness in the household is a high indicator of whether or not you are going to be impoverished. A quick survey of poor fatherless children at father. com, shows that children in father-absent homes are almost four times more likely to be poor.

Characteristics of a Famine and Poverty Spirit

So what do the famine spirit and the poverty spirit have to do with spiritual fathers and breaking the bastard spirit?

First, we need to look at what the behavior of a father operating under a famine or poverty spirits looks like. One of the most dominant behaviors we continue to see is instilling a spirit of competition amongst sons. The goal of such competition is not to groom their sons for success, but to perpetuate the illusion that resources are scarce, and to keep them in constant fear of losing them forever. Doom and destruction lurk around the corner. Fear is the motivator. If the fathers have a poverty mentality, they believe that resources are limited and since, they've had to work so hard for them, why should their sons get this for nothing? If the resources have dwindled, they will be difficult to get back. This mentality is actually underpinned by greed – in other words, I need more for my own consumption so there's not enough to go round.

Another behavior of a father operating under the spirit of either famine or poverty is an aversion to failure. Famine says, "If you fail, it's over – you'll never get another chance." Poverty says, "Why risk failure when things are just fine the way they are? Why strive for something that's uncertain?" Both mindsets prevent fathers from being good spiritual providers and increasing their sons' productivity and inheritance. As a pastors and leaders, the more we learn, the more we can pass on to the next generation.

Another factor that plays into whether or not you fall for the poverty spirit is the way you've been educated. Education in the natural world is a tool which allows people to rise out of their economic circumstances and gain the skills, knowledge and abilities to become self reliant. Education is a critical factor in the spiritual realm, too: people perish for lack of knowledge (Hosea 4:6). In other words, to break the poverty spirit I need to retrain my mind (Romans 12:3). I need to forget the lies and false mindsets I've been taught and learn the correct mindsets that the Lord has to teach me; mindsets that have God's mind have no problem with me being prosperous and scriptures abound that address that. Our God does not see profit as carnal and He doesn't call money evil. It is the love of money which is the root of all evil (1 Timothy 6:10).

We truly believe that God wants to fund the next great revival through His children. Therefore fathers and sons need to have that poverty mindset broken off of them!

The fat and lean cows

When we first read about Joseph and Pharaoh, he is summoned by Pharaoh to interpret the two kinds of cows in Pharaoh's dream, fat cows and skinny ones (Genesis 41:1-4). The fat cows represent poverty and the skinny cows represent famine. Satisfied as they look, the fat cows represent poverty in times of plenty, so while these cows eat, they eat not just to sustain themselves but, because they just can't get enough, they eat out of greed, lack wisdom and lack of provision for the lean years they expect to come. What they can no longer eat, they hoard. Both greed and hoarding are wasteful. They appear to be antithetical to one another but essentially they come from the same poverty spirit. On the one hand, greed makes you eat and eat beyond being satisfied for fear that there will be nothing tomorrow. Hoarding, on the other, makes you heap up things in containers in case one day there is lack, even if what you store has limited value.

Then in Pharaoh's dream, the skinny cows eat the fat cows because, no matter what they eat, the skinny cows, too, can never be satisfied. They have gone too long without a meal and have to eat everything in sight because starvation is just around the corner. Extreme famine will cause you to eat your own kind. Cows don't normally eat cows, and the church needs to stop eating its own out of the famine spirit. While the poverty spirit is motivated by greed and hoarding in times of plenty, the famine spirit devours everything in its path for fear of the lack overtaking it.

Famine and poverty can work together and in many areas they crisscross. The goal is to come out of both and to have the mindset of a kingdom wealth builder!

Jesus clearly differentiated the kingdom mindset from the poverty and famine mindset in the parable of the talents:

"He also who had received the one talent came forward, saying, 'Master, I knew you to be a hard man, reaping where you did not sow, and gathering where you scattered no seed, so I was afraid, and I went and hid your talent in the ground. Here, you have what is yours.' But his master answered him, 'You wicked and slothful servant! You knew that I reap where I have not sown and gather where I scattered no seed?'" (Matthew 25:24-26)

Here, Jesus shows us a servant who is operating under both the poverty and famine spirit working against the kingdom wealth mindset. The story goes as follows: a master is going on a long trip and gives his three servants money. To the first he gives five talents, to the second he gives two talents and to the last He gives one talent. We're going to focus on the guy who is given one talent for just a moment. The first two servants go and double their money. They understand the value of using money as a tool and they understand who they serve. But that last guy who only received one talent does something very strange: he buries (hoards) it in the dirt. I don't think this dude truly understands how seeds work. You can plant an acorn but not a coin. His belief is, there will be no more resources should he fail. He doesn't see money as the tool it's meant to be. Rather, his mentality is this, "When this money is gone, it's all over and because of the master's lack of love, I will get into huge trouble if I lose it and be left in lack."

How do we know the servant is fearful of his master? Well, he straight up tells him, "I know you are a harsh man and that you reap where you do not sow." He is literally accusing the master, "Not only are you mean but you are a thief! You're a shady guy who does shady dealings and takes harvests that aren't yours." When a son operates in the poverty and famine mindset, he fears and lacks trust in any investment. But more serious than that is his serious doubt of the good intentions of his father.

Pastor Terry was plagued with this parable for so many years that it even made him question the reliability of the scriptures. If the parable of the talents is like the kingdom of God, then the master represents Jesus. And that bothered Pastor Terry. How could Jesus reap where He didn't sow and make us believe that He was still good? One day while Pastor Terry was praying, the Lord spoke to him: "The accusation is true! I reaped where I did not sow. I never sowed the seeds of sin but I did reap the harvest of death." Wow! Jesus reaped what He did not sow! This didn't make Him mean; it makes Him merciful.

And so these twin demonic spirits of poverty and famine will ultimately try to have you buy into the lie that Jesus is not good. He is a mean master and only gave you a talent to have a reason to judge you for failing. The lie is that God will punish you for lack of perfection. If I'm not perfect, He'll punish me. He wants to take it from me. Dear sons and fathers, please know God loves you so much that He GAVE you His life and TOOK your punishment.

The poverty spirit says, "What I hold on to is mine." But Jesus says:

"Do not lay up for yourselves treasures on earth, where moth and rust destroy and where thieves break in and steal, but lay up for yourselves treasures in heaven, where neither moth nor rust destroys and where thieves do not break in and steal. For where your treasure is, there your heart will be also" (Matthew 6:19-21).

Whatever you hold on to, whatever stays as yours in this natural world rusts, rots, decays and is stolen. But what's His remains. When He gives you resources and you hold on to them, you activate the natural law of decay. But, when you allow what He gives you to remain His, as in the case of the two servants who viewed the talents as still belonging to the master – then it cannot decay. The one that held on to the talent didn't fully understand who owned it to take the risk of investing it. A closed fist cannot receive anything new. You must open your hands and release what you carry to receive something more. The poverty spirit doesn't want you to trust God as the owner who, as He directs you, will cause it to grow. The poverty spirit goes against the first foundational command: "Be fruitful and multiply" (Genesis 1:28). Our God is a fruitful God who sees His creation multiply. He created you to be the same, a person who is fruitful and multiplies His gifts.

The story of the talents is essentially all of our story. In fact, I would go so far as to say that the story of the talents in its original state had nothing to do with money. Money is just one expression of the talents just like money is only one expression of the poverty spirit. Money is the contemporary example in Jesus' day but in the beginning it was something very different and much more valuable.

> *...then the Lord God formed the man of dust from the ground and breathed into his nostrils the breath of life, and the man became a living creature* (Genesis 2:7).

The master in Jesus' story gives a coin but the first object of value God the Master and Creator gave man was not a coin *but a spirit.* It was the most valuable asset imaginable: the gift of His spirit. He gave it to us and then issued the first command, "Be fruitful and multiply."

His spirit is more valuable than gold or silver; it is the treasure of all treasures and it is given to each one of us with the same command, "Be fruitful and multiply." When we come to Jesus, we activate and bring to life that which remained dormant in us: His spirit. We are called to multiply that which we have been given. The first multiplication is to multiply His spirit. It's not just the Great Commission, the last command to go out and see spirits reconciled to God. It is His first command:

"You shall love the Lord your God with all your heart and with all your soul and with all your mind. This is the great and first commandment. And a second is like it: You shall love your neighbor as yourself" (Matthew 22:37-39).

When we bring people to Jesus, we fulfill the two greatest commandments: Love God and love others. We fulfill the Great Commission, "Go and make disciples of all nations." We also fulfill the first command, "Be fruitful and multiply." We need to multiply His sons and daughters on the earth, to awaken the spirit of God in them. Yet, sadly, ninety-five percent of all Christians have never won a soul to Christ. NEVER! ninety-nine percent of ministries believe they are commanded to evangelize, yet they simply do not.

Let us look at the talents as our spirits. What catastrophic harm are we wielding on our own spirits by burying our spirits and not multiplying them? We get saved and then we bury our faith in our own hearts and never give it away or invest it in others. We make no investment and therefore see no multiplication in others. Our spirits begin to rot, rust and decay until we are left with a warped and twisted perspective of Christianity – totally self-centered. We have been allowing the poverty spirit to tell us, "Just make it through life with your faith intact and don't worry about others – they will just try to steal your joy and peace and taint your faith. Isolate yourself and bury yourself away from the world so they cannot rob you of your goodness."

We miss the truth that we were meant to multiply the righteousness of God we carry inside, and multiply the grace of God on our own lives. You see, the poverty spirit doesn't just want to steal your financial increase; it wants to steal your faith increase as well. It doesn't just want to steal your money; it wants to steal your miracles. It's not just about your funds; it's about your future. It's about their future, too – all those you were empowered and commanded to reach and bring to life. When you fulfill the command to bring life to them, you deal death to the poverty spirit over you.

The poverty spirit will always try to convince you that God's resources are rationed to keep you from stepping out on God's word. If He directs it, He will provision it. There cannot be a lack when God gives it to you. Learn to become a steward, instead of an owner of it. Your willingness to give it back when asked will always lead to Him giving you more to manage and steward.

Don't figure

It's funny how, when we receive a direction from God, we think we need to figure out how to finance it. Peter fished all night and caught nothing but, when Jesus told him to cast his net again, they were filled. Peter didn't have to figure out the best financing method. He just needed to be obedient to His Master's voice. You can't out clever God. God is not sitting back saying, "I have a plan for you but I need you to figure out how to make it successful." No, just throw your net out when and where He says and it will return fruitful and multiplied because His word does not return to Him void (Isaiah 55:11). Obey His command by understanding that all of it belongs to Him anyway: that will smash the stronghold of poverty right out of your life.

Change your thinking. Take tithing, for example. The poverty spirit says God wants ten percent of my resources. The kingdom spirit says God has provided me all my resources and lets me keep ninety percent of what He produced for me. We co-labor with Him and we keep the bulk of the increase!

That is a perspective shift. Even collaborating in writing this book is breaking the poverty spirit. The poverty spirit says, "I can't stop to help my fellow brother or I may not get my tasks done." The kingdom mindset understands that working together always brings an exponential increase, not just a doubling. Ever try to move a large piece of furniture by yourself, scooting it one end at a time? It could take you an hour to get it out of the house. Have another friend grab the other side and what takes up all your time now just takes a moment. We worked together on this and realized very quickly that our revelation together was so much deeper – literally iron sharpening iron!

The poverty spirit competes for resources against brothers believing the father's inheritance will be taken by the other. While many of us love the Lord and have an intimate and meaningful relationship with God, many times we are still competing against our brothers much like Jacob and Esau. Did you know you can be a good son and a bad sibling? The poverty mindset sees brothers as opposition instead of encouragement, competitors instead of companions.

Ren's dad suffered from this spirit. He would grow a large business, only to see it ultimately fail time and time again. As it would grow, he would not hire the help he needed. If he did hire someone, he paid them poverty wages and never had the quality people he needed. Why? To hold on to HIS resources. He didn't want to give up a dime. As a result, he actually lost business in his retail store due to bad service and lazy workers. His retail store was a mess; things would be disorganized and chaotic. It was too much for him alone and he refused to hire people with the skills and expertise he lacked – in management, technology and inventory organization. So every business venture would actually fail because it grew too big for him to steward alone.

See your brothers in Christ as assets, not obstacles. The poverty spirit believes wealth is the greatest resource when the kingdom mindset knows that *wisdom* is. Wisdom can create wealth but wealth can never make you wise. The poverty mindset cannot grow wealth because it over values it.

> *Blessed is the one who finds wisdom, and the one who gets understanding, for the gain from her is better than gain from silver and her profit better than gold. She is more precious than jewels, and nothing you desire can compare with her. Long life is in her right hand; in her left hand are riches and honor* (Proverbs 3:13-16).

Learn to partner with people instead of pausing in the poverty mindset. Release sons and provision them with wisdom and resources, and you will see it return to you.

> *Honor the Lord with your wealth and with the firstfruits of all your produce; then your barns will be filled with plenty, and your vats will be bursting with wine* (Proverbs 3:9-10).

Pastors and people reading this, find anointed sons and other ministries, and partner with them instead of trying to duplicate what they are called and anointed for. To the pastors reading this that are waiting on God's people to start giving, what you model will manifest. Don't ask people to do what you are unwilling to do. In order to break free, start giving freely into people and ministries that you don't own or have no part in. Many pastors, on the one hand, want people to give to a ministry that those people have no ownership in but, on the other, those same pastors only give into what they control.

Control is a characteristic of both the poverty mindset and famine spirit. I hear it all the time. When things don't go as we hoped or expected, we make the statement, "God is in control." We just had an election while writing this, and my social media feed is full of disappointed people whose candidate didn't win and they are consoling themselves with the statement that God is in control. I think this makes them feel better that they had no real power to change the circumstance they are in. The poverty mindset therefore says, "Why try? You have no authority because God controls everything." This is not scriptural. In fact it is exactly the opposite. God handed dominion over to man in the garden and He expects us to exercise that authority.

All you have to do is look around at the world to see if God is in control of it. By the evil and pain in the world, we can easily conclude either He is not in control or He is not good. If He was, the world would look quite different, we think. So, because we believe He is in control, we unwittingly have bought into the lie that He is not good.

The truth is God commands, not controls.

He gives us His commands and we are in control of whether we obey or not. God commanded that Egypt let His people go but Moses had to obey that command by using that staff that worked miracles. Pharoah disobeyed the command of God, and plagues and death were the result. So many of the stories of the bible involve sons who disobeyed. They had the free will to choose not to obey the command of God. There are consequences for it like any good parent will tell you. The reason we are correcting this, is that by allowing this misunderstanding to fester, it will give room to these mindsets that will rob your spiritual resources.

To His sons: God does not control us but He does command us. He does not condemn us but He does correct us. He is good and, if we hear and obey His commands, we will see His goodness shine through our circumstances. To see how truly loving God is toward us, all we have to do is look to His two greatest commands: love God and love others. Not just love God but the other children He loves, too. This loving God commanded us to care for orphans and widows. He is good and, when we obey, we see that goodness. A sign of that goodness is not having to worry about lack. He wants you to rely on His commands to be full of His presence and provision. The more we focus on obeying His command to love, the more we see Him break the power of poverty and meet every need – we have to be able to just love more.

Commanders lead the army; their soldiers fight with them. They grow authority through loyalty. Tyrants use control and intimidation to hold on to their power. Bad fathers control; good fathers command.

Poverty Spirit vs the Poor in Spirit

"Blessed are the poor in spirit, for theirs is the kingdom of heaven" (Matthew 5:3).

All of heaven's spiritual principles have both an earthly fulfillment and an opposite demonic counterpart. You may have read the scripture above and somehow believe that it must negate our premise. Remember the enemy knows the scriptures, too. He is notorious for using the scriptures out of context, where he applies the opposite demonic deliverance of true spiritual principles.

The enemy wants to rob you where heaven wants to reward you.

This verse in Matthew highlights a godly version of this spiritual truth. The poverty spirit is the enemy's twisting of the concept of poor in spirit and, while it may seem we are just splitting hairs, we are actually unmasking the deceptive tactics of the enemy.

Many people apply this scripture to our physical circumstances. They try to make the case that God loves poor people and doesn't like the rich. However, this scripture is not talking about the material world in any sense. How do we know that? Well, the "in spirit" part might be a clue. So, if God is not talking about the material world then, what is this truth He was attempting to share with the 5000 people gathered in the open that day?

When you are poor you have no resources, no land or houses. If you are poor you have no ability to store an excess of resources. The Hebrews had none of these in the wilderness but God gave them their daily manna from heaven to sustain them as they wandered in the desert.

Then the Lord said to Moses, "I will rain down bread from heaven for you. The people are to go out each day and gather enough for that day. In this way I will test them and see whether they will follow my instructions. On the sixth day they are to prepare what they bring in, and that is to be twice as much as they gather on the other days" (Exodus 16:4-5 NIV).

God rained down daily bread to sustain them. They could collect all they needed but they had to collect it before the day was hot, or it would melt away. Remember, the manna could not be kept overnight. It would go rancid if they tried to save it. Except the sabbath. God would sustain the manna to last two days on the sabbath every week. So why did God want the children to rely on this food from heaven? We learn more in Deuteronomy.

He humbled you, causing you to hunger and then feeding you with
manna, which neither you nor your ancestors had known, to teach
you that man does not live on bread alone but on every word that
comes from the mouth of the Lord (Deuteronomy 8:3 NIV).

God did not want the Hebrews storing the provision, so each day
they would have to trust God all over again. They would have to
see that the source of their provision was God. Jesus mirrored this
deep spiritual truth in the Lord's prayer, "Give us our daily bread"
– our daily bread, our manna, the spiritual food He provides.
So "poor in spirit" simply means you are completely spiritually
reliant on the Lord to supply the miracle, the joy, the peace and,
for that, you need a fresh supply daily. It's new every morning.
God did not create you to hoard up His relationship, to hoard up
His love, hoard up His peace and joy. You are to trust Him that, if
He met your need yesterday, then He will surely do it today.

"Poor in spirit" means we pour out our spirit;
we empty out everyday.

If He pours love into us, then we need to use that resource that day
or risk it going rancid. We are meant to use it and pour it out. The
secret to getting more, is simply giving more. When you're giving
away your resources, then you will truly need more of them daily
to sustain you. Blessed are the poor in spirit, those that trust Him
to supply today's need and have no intention of trying to store it
up. If you have to go to Him daily, then He knows He can grow
you in spirit and have intimacy with you. Open you hand and
release the joy, peace, healing, prayers, finances, and anointing
that you carry so He can give you more.

You can see this contrast in full display in people's relationships.
Those that have a poverty mindset will try to hoard and store love

from you. They will want you to be their only friend. They will guilt you if they feel left out and hurt by your other friendships. They will get jealous when you pour out love on others because they believe there will not be enough. It's always about trying to remove anything that could take away from their supply. We see this in ministry all the time. People become jealous of ministers connecting to their friends. They fear being left out. The poverty spirit invites the fear of famine to set in. On the other hand, the poor in spirit trust God to supply everything they need and they know that, if they have a relationship need, they can just go and get their daily supply, Him.

The poverty spirit goes beyond people and spills over in places it never belongs, church. Ministers are so afraid of working together because their members may like the other pastor more and go to their church instead. This is the ultimate ministry example of the poverty mindset. There is a true lack of belief that God is the supplier of the manna, the people, the resources and, if you use it, then God will bring more. Instead they hold it and it goes rancid. We need to learn how to be blessed by being poor in spirit. Let it go; you don't have any way to hold on to it and store it anyway. Poor people can only take what they can carry. Is it possible that God is trying to lighten our burden?

Can you imagine a marathon runner trying to store up hydration? He takes a backpack full of water and has bottles taped around him, measuring exactly what water he will need with him for the race. Storing all that water becomes a burden. How would he do? Will he win? Of course not! He has to trust that as he needs water that there will be water stations and people along the way that will supply what is needed, when it is needed, and he has no concern but to run his race. Wow, what a picture of the poor in spirit! Trust, peace, and swiftness are added to those that understand. The poor in spirit mindset is meant to bless you into laying down those heavy burdens. You can't carry them and you shouldn't try. He will supply all your needs.

The poverty spirit wants you to store, hoard and weigh yourself down in areas God has called you just to trust Him. Store where God tells you to store. Trust Him to supply all the rest.

The famine spirit is broken by eating spiritual bread daily, while the poverty spirit can be broken by simply being grateful for the bread you are given by God. Breaking these twin spirits is in the ability to count your blessings and trust that He will always provide.

Eating bread daily is a principle that applies in the natural as well. Let's look at the marathon runner again. One of the interesting techniques a good marathon coach will teach you is not just that you need to eat and drink but, if you wait to eat till you are hungry, it's too late. If you wait to drink, till you are thirsty, it's too late. You drink and eat on a timed schedule to make sure you can maintain your energy levels and keep your body intact. We should be hungry and thirsty after the Lord but we shouldn't wait to seek Him till we feel that hunger and thirst. We seek Him whether we "feel like it" or not.

CHAPTER 6

A WARNING TO THE HOUSE OF ELI

Eli is ultimately a tragic tale of a father who had so much potential but allowed fear and neglect to rob him of legacy and lineage. Eli was a great spiritual father to Samuel but was a terrible father to his own biological boys. At the time of Samuel's encounter with God, Eli's sons were committing fornication in the tabernacle; they were stealing from God; they were threatening the people. This was not a secret; it was well-known amongst the people.

However, Eli reneged on his parental duties. He did not punish his sons because he was afraid of them. When a spiritual father allows fear to come into his life, he begins to lose his spiritual vision. Eli could have impacted the outcome of his story by simply demanding that his boys leave their priestly rolls and repent. But instead he remained silent.

I believe Eli and the house of Eli have risen in this generation and they occupy major roles in the Christian Movement. Modern day Elis look like woke pastors. They speak uplifting inspirational self-help messages. They have opinions on every social justice issue but never on self sin issues. Not every message has to cover this issue, of course. You don't have to be a hell fire and brimstone preacher but, if a pastor's message never challenges you to grow and fix the brokenness you have, then you may have an Eli on your hands. A well rounded church's goal should not be to make you feel better about being broken but should equip you to be mended.

Pastor Terry is a church planter who is multi-vocational or, as he likes to joke, has several jobs to pay for his church planting hobby. One of these many jobs is cleaning a church. A week before beginning to write this book, he was cleaning and began to feel a heaviness come on him. Terry began to pray in tongues and, by the time he had finished cleaning, he began to hear in his spirit one sentence over and over: "Judgment is coming to the house of Eli." Terry does not believe necessarily this word was for the church he cleans, but that God was putting a warning out to His bride.

One of the characteristics of a spiritual father who is an Eli is complacency towards sin. When a spiritual father is afraid to speak against sin, the house quickly becomes corrupted by the spiritual sons of Eli. Often, the spirit of Eli rises up in liters from what seems like a good place. I don't want to offend people and come across as unloving, so I will talk carefully about sin. Pastors have even begun to speak more about grace than about the need for repentance because they want to present a super loving Jesus. After all, Jesus is a very loving leader. Part of the problem we have in our generation is that certain sins are now considered identity issues. Therefore, if you come against the sin, you're coming against a person's identity.

The world is crying out, why can't you accept me as I am but, in doing so, they also demand that God changes who He is. Sin separates us from our God-given identity because we are made in the image of God. God is not *sinful*! He is holy and pure. The idea that your identity is found in sin would mean that God created you to be sinful or that God is not concerned about the effects of sin. So a pastor would look at this conundrum and feel like it will be unloving to speak of sin.

Recently I was chewed out by a woman after speaking openly about the sin of abortion being murder. She believed that, because Christians have in the past presented this argument unlovingly; they were immoral and at risk of hurting the feelings of those who committed abortion. In other words, if you preach against abortion you are bringing condemnation on women who've had an abortion. I explained to her that I always open the conversation with the grace of God to those who have committed the sin of abortion and that they can have the guilt and shame of their decision removed from their life. But murder is always murder.

Her view was that it would be better if Christians would just stay out of the abortion conversation because it comes across as offensive to people who are newly coming into the church. This would be a moment in which an Eli would find a way not to speak of the sin lest he upset his congregation. Again, the goal in preaching about sin is not to bring condemnation but to highlight a path to redemption through repentance. I love you too much to allow you to sin your way to hell.

By the way, our very loving Jesus taught a lot on "Hell." Out of the 162 references to hell in the bible, 70 are from a very loving Jesus. Elis say, "Choose the battles you want to die for wisely." Well, Jesus died for the battle over sin and has won. If pastors refuse to preach on sin, they are leaving a door open for their spiritual sons to become sinful. I would also ask any pastor who says their goal is to be seeker-friendly – and therefore don't preach on sin or hell – if they are willing to allow the Holy Spirit to judge their motives. It's easy to tell everyone we are motivated by love and consideration for people, while simultaneously being motivated by fear and desire for reputation.

In our day, one of the alarming products of the house of Eli has been the rise of woke pastors. Woke pastors follow social justice issues instead of God's justice system. Woke pastors march in step with popular movements but stay quiet about lawlessness against the kingdom of God. A woke pastor will present messages that will make congregations feel warm and fuzzy. It inspires them to become better people through self-help. But the problem with any virtue that has the word "self" in front of the virtue is that it's ultimately a form of idolatry. Self-worth, self-reliance, and self-esteem can be easy strongholds for the idolizing of oneself or one's opinions – which is idolatry.

When you increase the crowd, you decrease the individual.

When we worship ourselves, we also believe we have the right to judge ourselves according to crowd behavior instead of the Word of God. We tend to overlook our own sin because, ultimately, we believe we're not as bad as that guy. This leads to self-righteousness. We have to walk in godly humility. Many times we find ourselves making an effort to avoid this pridefulness, flipping to the other extreme. At the same time, if you are worried you might be in pride over your overly weighted self-worth, you may flip to the other extreme of self-loathing. That's called false humility and it can be as dangerous as pride. In fact, it is the other side of the same coin of pride. Ultimately, self adulation or self hatred are still founded on looking at self instead of keeping our eyes on God.

How do we avoid falling into pride or false humility? Simple: understand exactly what humility is. Here is the definition. **Perfect humility is understanding and walking out exactly who God has created you to be, nothing more, nothing less.** Godly identity is perfect humility. This only comes from a relationship with God; He has to fill you in on this identity.

The spiritual father's job is to help you find your identity. The house of Eli doesn't validate their identity from God but rather they get their identity from outside validators. Crowds are a big motivator to the House of Eli. Crowds provide the cover and validation, which should mainly come from a father. Crowds offer a covering from having to make a decision or a stand. Crowds, by their very nature, are neither moral or immoral, but historically they are terrible at knowing good. So, if a hard stance is required, a leader can announce that they don't want to be unloving and decide to stay quiet – and the crowd will be happy.

Crowds cannot be Crowds if they are composed of individuals because individuals will always stand out. Let us illustrate this. I want you to watch as a crowd forms around Jesus and how they react when a blind man who is desperate for a touch from Jesus begins to cry out!

> *As he drew near to Jericho, a blind man was sitting by the roadside begging. And hearing a crowd going by, he inquired what this meant. They told him, "Jesus of Nazareth is passing by." And he cried out, "Jesus, Son of David, have mercy on me!" And those who were in front rebuked him, telling him to be silent. But he cried out all the more, "Son of David, have mercy on me!"* (Luke 18:35-39)

You must understand at this point in Jesus' ministry, there are stories already going around everywhere of all of the healings that

Jesus has done. So is it safe to say that what the crowd is doing is completely and totally unloving? They try to silence a blind man who is yelling loudly and are keeping him from the healing he needs. Are you telling me that no one in the crowd had ever heard that Jesus had healed blind people, raised the dead, cleansed the lepers, or walked on water? The problem always comes about when individuals make crowds uncomfortable.

This is where one of the problems arises in finding cover in the crowd. The cover is at the cost of allowing Jesus to be Jesus and for desperate people to seek Him. The man shouting for Jesus has a desperate need but it's shining a problem on the belief and the motivation of the crowd. We cannot allow our desire to "act right" within the crowd prevent us from seeking after God with all desperation. One man came with a desperation for transformation. The rest of the crowd just came for information.

The other problem with finding cover in the crowd is that the crowd is easily swayed. Jesus in verse 40 stops the crowd and commands the blind man to come near Him. Jesus brings the blind man out of the crowd and heals his blindness.

Instantly he could see again. His eyes popped opened, and he saw Jesus. He shouted loud praises to God and he followed Jesus. And when the crowd saw what happened, they too erupted with shouts of praise to God (Luke 18:43 TPT).

Notice, one minute the crowd is scolding the blind man by telling him to be quiet so they can watch Jesus pass by, but the very next minute they're excited and celebrating with the blind man. Our generation needs leaders to be called out of the crowd and have their blindness healed; but it will cost you leaving the cover of the crowd.

If you read on to Luke 19, you'll see the crowd is about to change its mind once more. Jesus pulls Zacchaeus out of a tree and invites Himself to his house to eat. You see once again the crowd was blocking Zacchaeus, a very short man, from seeing the Savior. So, out of desperation, Zacchaeus finds a place above the crowd. It is interesting that Jesus is calling Zacchaeus to come down from that tree, a place he didn't belong.

Zacchaeus is called out of the tree to meet Jesus, yet Jesus was called on to a tree to meet us.

Then the crowd turns. When the crowd finds out that Jesus is going to a Tax Collector's house, they stop rejoicing about Jesus healing a blind man and start complaining about Him eating with sinners. They were good with Jesus healing the sick but they were not forgiving of the sinful. If Jesus had been worried about the crowd, He would have found a more reputable home to dine in. He could have met privately with Zacchaeus to save Himself from "dealing" with the poor optics.

Woke Leaders always find a way to justify shunning people who don't fit into the crowd. They call it Cancel Culture: "Zacchaeus is a traitor to his people. He is an oppressor and a thief." The crowd has a right to dislike Zacchaeus but the crowd isn't behaving like Jesus. Zacchaeus has an encounter with Jesus and receives salvation and repays all his thievery. What an incredible moment that must have been, yet sadly we hear no mention of the crowd rejoicing.

Ren set a goal on Sundays as a measuring rod of how he was doing and to protect him from the sway of the crowd. First, he recognized that Sunday morning was not the church but the crowd. The church is the one that sticks around asking more questions even when the crowds have left. They show up for small groups and leadership training. They show up on cleaning day and come early to get the coffee ready. Those are the church. Second, the crowd's opinion didn't validate his success. He determined, if all he got after his message were handshakes and, "Well done todays," then he'd missed the mark. Instead he looked for lives transformed. Who was healed? Who was saved? Who was restored? That's less visible and would easily get missed by the crowd.

Dear Woke Pastors, please be aware that your covering and validation need to come from your Father and not the crowd. If validation and covering come from the crowd, then you will always be led by the crowd instead of leading the crowd. Notice how unconcerned Jesus was with the crowd's opinion. Jesus knew how to build giant crowds; yet He would always do the will of His Father even when it meant the crowd would go home and turn their back on Him. It is important for the house of Eli to realize that the giant crowd that cheered when Jesus healed the Blind Man's eyes and fed 5000 people were probably the same crowd that yelled, "Crucify Him!" We want to see our churches and ministries draw in large crowds, for the inheritance of nations is for the sons of God. But the crowd can't become our motivation or validation because, if it turns, our identity will be lost. We are not giving you keys to grow a large church, we are giving you keys to grow the kingdom.

We can't afford the cost of sons of Eli running rampant.

Now the sons of Eli were worthless men. They did not know the Lord. The custom of the priests with the people was that when any man offered sacrifice, the priest's servant would come, while the meat was boiling, with a three-pronged fork in his hand,

and he would thrust it into the pan or kettle or cauldron or pot.
All that the fork brought up the priest would take for himself.
This is what they did at Shiloh to all the Israelites who came
there. Moreover, before the fat was burned, the priest's servant
would come and say to the man who was sacrificing, "Give meat
for the priest to roast, for he will not accept boiled meat from
you but only raw." And if the man said to him, "Let them burn
the fat first, and then take as much as you wish," he would say,
"No, you must give it now, and if not, I will take it by force."
Thus the sin of the young men was very great in the sight of the
Lord, for the men treated the offering of the Lord with contemp
(1 Samuel 2:12).

Eli didn't correct his sons and they became worthless men who
didn't fear God. What is worse is who became their father. The
Hebrew bible says in verse 12 that they were sons of Belial who
didn't know God. How is it possible that Eli raised two biological
sons that didn't know the Lord? I do not doubt that Eli was a good
man who loved the Lord and followed the priestly instructions.
So some assumptions must be made in order to understand how
Eli's sons had become the worthless men that they were. One
assumption would be that somehow Eli chose not to instruct
his boys in Levitical law or that they just didn't understand the
expectations. But this would require you to believe that they
could be placed in a position as priests without knowledge of
expectations. This seems very unlikely.

Therefore, it's not out of the realm of possibility that, after the
sons became priests, they slowly begin to make sinful decisions.
Without anyone correcting them, they continued down this
path and began hardening their heart to the sanctity of the place
because they no longer feared the wrath of God. They may even
have believed that their ceremonial cleaning and sacrifices were

enough to cover their habitual sin. We see this in the modern day church with those who live a form of hyper grace in which they no longer fear the Lord and do what they wish, relying solely on grace to remove all judgment.

Ultimately, because a spiritual father never corrected the wayward sons, they began bringing mixture to the house of the Lord. They placed themselves over God and did not even honor the sacrifices on the altar, taking from the sacrifice before it was given to God. They would steal from God and take devoted meat for sacrifice. The first step to profaneness and unrighteousness is a lack of fear of the Lord. Once you walk away from the fear of the Lord, you have no problem going into deeper levels of wickedness. Eli's sons went so far as to take advantage of the women who came to serve the Lord and they would fornicate with them. They used their position of authority to seduce women who came to the house of the Lord with the best intentions. Sadly, Eli had an opportunity from the very beginning to correct his sons and to allow them to walk a repentant lifestyle.

Repentance is not a bad word; it is the opportunity to experience God's grace and mercy in powerful ways. Pastors should not fear correcting their spiritual children. I believe some pastors are afraid to stop their spiritual children and talk to them about the need for repentance for fear they will get upset and leave the church. The church desperately needs to repent of the sins of mixture, fornication and theft of the Gospel. We need a pure and spotless bride who is not allowed New Age self-help to replace repentance, grace and mercy.

However, when an "Eli" is socially aware of his or her popularity, he will also overlook the sins of his spiritual sons. God always detests mixture and fornication in His tabernacle. But, when there are no spiritual fathers to speak against the sins of their sons, the sins will run rampant.

We believe God is opening a season of exposure. This season has to happen, not because God hates His sons, but because He loves them too much to let them continue to die in their sin. This exposure is happening at every level in government, business, the media and in the church. One of the products of this exposure is that, as the Elis and the sons of Eli are exposed, there will be a rise of Samuels who will begin to bring forth the revelation of the Lord.

As leaders, we have to be very careful not to find ourselves replicating the same behavior as Eli. Eli was a good spiritual father to Samuel but he was derelict in his duty to his own children. Unfortunately, we see the same ultimate outcome in Samuel's life. Samuel is a force to be reckoned with. In today's terms, Samuel would say, "I might be saved but I'm not soft!" However, even though he is bold enough to stand up to kings, we see his own sons repeat the pattern of Eli's sons. As Samuel ages, he appoints his sons as judges, only to see them turn corrupt and greedy. The errors of Eli echo back at Samuel. No solution or reasoning is given other than that his sons simply did not follow his ways (1 Samuel 8:1-9).

What we model will multiply.

As fathers, it's important to raise sons up by our example. "Do as I say, not as I do" is as flawed then and it is now. I've seen it too many times. If spiritual sons can carry the spiritual fathers' blessing and anointing, that means they can also carry the same curse.

When your primary motivation is to be liked by those you lead, whether sons or crowds, you will ultimately find yourself being led by them, and when they turn, you may find yourself in a Jesus situation where they just want to throw you off a cliff. Small church pastors know this all too well. They took the appointment wanting to be world changers; but just ask them if they would survive changing the weekly bulletin or adding some lights to the stage. Their message last Sunday was their best but they wouldn't survive a new song suggestion. Politicians may be swayed by the polls, but priests and kings should stand on the rock of Jesus, the rock of His Word. So, whether no one sees what you carry or thousands gather to receive from you, live for the approval of one person: God alone. A good spiritual father will remind his sons of this and keep them laser pointed on this target.

CHAPTER 7

COUNTERFEIT FATHERS VERSUS TRUE FATHERS

*The Son of God became a man to enable men to
become sons of God.*
-C.S. Lewis

When the world's spiritual fathers are better than the fathers of the children of God, then the church is truly in crisis. Satan loves to counterfeit God's creation. Satan only counterfeits that which has value. No one checks if a $1 bill is counterfeit because it doesn't have enough value to counterfeit. Spiritual fathers have kingdom value and the crisis comes when Satan's counterfeits start to look better than the church's products. We cannot allow the world's spiritual fathers to be more accepting, loving, forgiving and committed than God's appointed fathers. Each time, we who are called, abandon a son who is called, we mar, tarnish, and deform the image he was created to become.

One of the things we need to understand about Satan is that he is, like us, a created being. But unlike us, he is not made in God's image and does not have His breath in him. Therefore, he has no creative abilities like the Father. The ultimate tool that he will use is an imitation of God's creation. The goal would be to take that which the Heavenly Father has created, and imitate it, undermine it and give it a false image.

To see how all this plays out, let us look at two case studies, Pharaoh and Abraham.

Pharaoh - the Counterfeit Father

The counterfeit father can clearly be seen in the story of Joseph. Joseph has a father who loves him and has seen Joseph's leadership abilities. Joseph's father shows him favor and gives him a coat of many colors, which is seen by many scholars as a sign that Joseph is being given authority by his father. It would even explain the fact that Joseph is sent to check on his brothers by his father.

Joseph has two dreams, which he interprets to mean that he will be the ruler over his family. Not surprisingly, Joseph's brothers have become extremely jealous of their father's favor towards Joseph and annoyed with Joseph's Dreams. They succumb to the famine spirit which always suggests that resources are limited, including the father's love. This leads them into a murderous path in which they actually plot to kill their own brother.

And there begins the journey of Joseph from beloved son, to betrayed brother, to slave, to prisoner and, amazingly, at the end of it all, prince of Egypt. Pastors love to speak on Joseph's story, the highlight of which is when God takes Joseph from the pit and puts him in the palace. But, when you read the story, it would be helpful to understand that it has nothing to do with Joseph's journey to the palace. Rather, it has everything to do with the redemption and salvation of his family so that they could perpetuate the lineage which will lead to the prophesied Messiah.

Also, it's important to note that, when Joseph is in the palace, he's actually spiritually at risk. Here is the enemy doing his thing

102

– imitating the Father. While it's incredible that God can bring you up from the lowest pits of your life to the highest palaces, let's not forget that this palace was run by a king who believes himself to be the Sun King, son of God. So Pharaoh offers to Joseph the gift of a substitute father since his own father Israel is absent.

And Pharaoh said to his servants, "Can we find a man like this, in whom is the Spirit of God?" Then Pharaoh said to Joseph, "Since God has shown you all this, there is none so discerning and wise as you are. You shall be over my house, and all my people shall order themselves as you command. Only as regards the throne will I be greater than you."

And Pharaoh said to Joseph, "See, I have set you over all the land of Egypt." Then Pharaoh took his signet ring from his hand and put it on Joseph's hand, and clothed him in garments of fine linen and put a gold chain about his neck. And he made him ride in his second chariot. And they called out before him, "Bow the knee!" Thus he set him over all the land of Egypt. Moreover, Pharaoh said to Joseph, "I am Pharaoh, and without your consent no one shall lift up hand or foot in all the land of Egypt." And Pharaoh called Joseph's name Zaphenath-paneah. And he gave him in marriage Asenath, the daughter of Potiphera priest of On. So Joseph went out over the land of Egypt (Genesis 41:41-45).

Pharaoh, as the imitation father, is offering Joseph a ring of authority and is putting a new coat from his own wardrobe on him. Sounds familiar doesn't it? Pharaoh places a gold chain around his neck, then allows him to ride in his second chariot around Egypt with his attendants demanding that everyone kneel before Joseph. This sounds like a victory ride but it is a false fulfillment of the godly dream Joseph had when he was a kid.

Pharaoh even plays the role of name giver and changes his Hebrew name to Zaphenath-paneah after a pagan god. If you're reading the story and you can't see how Pharaoh is being a substitute father, ask Holy Spirit to open your eyes to discernment. This is one of the greatest tricks of the enemy: to offer you something good that isn't God, something that is the imitation rather than the real thing.

It's also interesting to note that at this time Joseph turns thirty, which is the same age that Jesus was when he started his ministry. Joseph is offered the kingdom of Egypt with only Pharaoh above him. At the same age, Jesus is offered the kingdoms of the earth by another king, the imitator, deceiver, and false father, whose name is Satan. All Satan wanted was for Jesus to trade fathers and for Satan to assume the role of Jesus' Pharaoh. *"All these I will give you if you will fall down and worship me"* (Matthew 4:9) is what he promises.

Most pastors preach that Joseph represents a Messianic promise in the Old Testament. The parallels with Jesus are obvious: a son with special love from his father, sold for silver, falsely accused, stripped of his robe and delivered up to the Gentiles etc. Again, the story never reveals a single sin in Joseph's life, though some may argue that Joseph was prideful in sharing his dream. But they don't understand prophetic promise. In order to activate a prophetic promise declared over your life, you must speak it and act on it. This moves it from *declared* to *decreed*. Something declared is a formal announcement but something decreed is a formal order under force of law. What was declared in a dream was decreed when Joseph spoke it into existence, and it activated the chain of events that would lead to the ultimate fulfillment of that prophetic promise.

As a bonus, if you have been speaking your prophetic promises and you haven't seen them manifest, take heart – you haven't been thrown in a pit by your brothers yet, so there's that consolation. Not every prophetic decree elevates you to the king's palace in the beginning. The prophetic has a process. As our friends at Global Awakening say, trust the process. Joseph's saving grace may have been that Joseph did, in fact, have a good father – they were separated by no fault of either one of them. So God used the positioning of Joseph to restore the true father, and the son brought salvation to his family. Today, God wants the hearts of the fathers returned to the sons (Malachi 4:6).

So, while Joseph was offered a false father, when a son has experienced a godly father's love, he can't help but reflect the image of that father. Similarly, sons of this generation are being given the choice of which father they will serve.

When a generation finds itself fatherless, the bastard spirit will try to fill its void with imitation. The enemy is all too happy to offer imitation for the void, and that could mean self-love, pride, lust of the flesh, and selfishness. All these will be their substitute guides to unwittingly build the kingdom of darkness.

King Saul operated as a bad father and unwittingly sent a godly son, David, to a heathen imitation kingdom. We read that the king of Gath was good to David. He never mistreated David in any way in contrast to Saul. He did all the things that a father should do: he gave David identity, provided him land, offered him loyalty and acceptance, gave him a future and a purpose. So this heathen king in a way was a good father but not a God father. So when the bastard spirit makes you an offer you can't refuse, you'd better refuse it. You will end up in a covenant with a lesser father and miss your destiny. David was called to be a godly king, not to serve under a heathen king.

So what does the bastard spirit offer as an imitation father? What does he do? Imitation fathers will offer self-help and will give versions of the truth; but they cannot offer *the* truth. Imitation fathers will show children a path to success that doesn't involve building biblical character, perseverance or morality. False fathers will use fear and manipulation to change the hearts of sons. Ultimately, a false father will give you a false name as Pharaoh did for Joseph, and try to derail God's plan for your life.

We believe this generation is crying out for the authentic. It's looking for the real and it's done settling for the fake. We are looking for godly fathers:

And he will turn the hearts of fathers to their children and the hearts of children to their fathers (Malachi 4:6).

Abraham -
The Surrogate Father

If we want to truly dive into the power of true spiritual fathers, there is no better case study than Abraham. Abraham could be called the first surrogate father. He carried the role of father for Lot before he became the natural father of Ishmael and Isaac.

Let me illustrate the point about a true father. Pastor Terry and his wife Nina started mentoring a young curly-haired eight-year-old girl who looked like the TV character Ruth Camden. Mentoring started simply by taking her to church, special trips to the movies and making sure she had school clothes. They would help her with homework and, when needed, she would spend weeks at a time at their house. After about two years into mentoring, Pastor Terry felt God was telling him that he was called to be her father.

Nina and he began having serious conversations on what this would look like and how they could afford a kid. Could they handle the extra responsibilities especially since they were newly married? Ultimately, they knew in their hearts that God was calling them to take the leap of faith. Step one was to ask the ten-year-old if she would be okay with them becoming her legal parents. Needless to say she said yes. The next step was to file all the legal paperwork to start the adoption process, which included notifying her legal parents that their rights were being terminated. This was a long drawn-out process which led to the final step. The entire family stood before the judge. The judge explained to Alyssa that receiving a legal name meant she would be a legal heir and would have the last name Cuthbertson. That also meant the new parents would now have the legal right to discipline her.

Terry believes that adoption shifted his perspective of what it means to be loved by our Heavenly Father. No matter how hard things got, no matter how much Alyssa would try to test their resolve never to abandon her, Terry and Nina refused to give up, even to this day. Terry even has a tattoo with the adoption symbol and her adoption date. When you adopt a son or daughter, it is not a temporary thing: you must stand up to the commitment. By doing so, you break the walls the bastard spirit tries to erect to loose the spirit of rejection on sons and daughters.

There is something so powerful about taking on a spiritual son that it changes the way we view our Heavenly Father's love for us. Think about how the Father is so determined to win back the creation He loves that He sends His Son Jesus to let both Jew and Gentile know that adoption is available. Then He's willing to pay the high price of adoption. When a child is adopted, they receive the last name of the legal father and legal rights to an inheritance. As spiritual fathers, we get to experience the same love and affection the Father feels for us His adopted children. This experience can lead to being better sons.

Abraham's heart is for sacrifice.

Abraham is an incredible father both in the natural and spiritual because of his heart for honoring God in building altars and making sacrifices. Everywhere he goes, the First Act of his is to build an altar. What is an altar? It's a place of slaughter and sacrifice, where blood is shed and death takes place as an act of worship to God. Once you develop a heart for the altar, you'll realize the beauty and power of it. Ultimately, Abraham is willing to bring his son Isaac to the altar to be a living sacrifice.

Today, you are being invited into Abraham's family as a son. This means you're being invited to live the life of a sacrificial lamb. This is only available if you will go to the altar. You will soon realize that altars are messy – blood is shed and fire consumes. The altar is also a place of repentance, so when a father has a heart to build an altar, he is providing a place where sons can receive repentance. Altars are places were things go to die. Let your pride, anger, pain, and sin die at the altar of God. We need more spiritual fathers who are altar builders, who teach the power of repentance and sacrifice. In the new covenant, the altar is also a place of giving thanks where the sacrifice of praise can be brought.

For Abraham, the altar is a Place of Promise. The literal act of making a sacrifice of praise is a huge step of faith and obedience. Abraham understands that the act of sacrificial praise brings promise into barren lands. The first altar Abraham builds is in Shechem immediately after God promises him he will have Offspring who will occupy the land of Canaan. Altars are also a place of Memorial and Remembrance, a place to bring the sacrifice of praise even when we have not yet seen the Fulfillment of the Promise.

> *Abram passed through the land to the place at Shechem, to the oak of Moreh. At that time the Canaanites were in the land. Then the Lord appeared to Abram and said, "**To your offspring I will give this land.**" So he built there an altar to the Lord, who had appeared to him. From there he moved to the hill country on the **east of Bethel** and pitched his tent, with Bethel*

on the west and Ai on the east. And there he built an altar to the Lord and called upon the name of the Lord (Genesis 12:6-7, emphasis added).

Notice that after the famine, Abraham left Egypt to return to Negev and sacrificed again at the former altar he had set up in Bethel (Genesis 13:3). The altar still stood and the promise still remained. Spiritual fathers who build altars take territory that becomes inheritance for their spiritual Sons. The legacy of teaching our spiritual Sons to become Lovers of the altar and Bringers of the sacrifice opens the door for our children to become spiritually enriched.

Abraham the provider

Abraham's ability to be an altar Builder also means he knows how to sacrificially give to his spiritual Sons. Abraham is focused on the Blesser not the blessing. He understands that, if he stays connected to his Heavenly Father, he will walk in abundance and therefore does not have to fight to hold on to any blessings that has been given to him. He can freely give them away. Naturally this Act of Giving helps Abraham to become very rich in livestock, silver and gold. Fathers who grow and become rich spiritually will also bring their spiritual children to a place where they will also walk in abundance.

Abraham is not the only one who's becoming rich; so is his surrogate son Lot. So when the herdsmen of Abraham and those of Lot begin to fight, Abraham can be a peacemaker by giving Lot the freedom to expand his territory. Abraham invites Lot to take any part of the land that he desires, even if it will cost Abraham. Lot naturally chases the blessing and takes what looks like the most desirable land, the fertile plain to the east.

I think this is a spiritual lesson that all leaders could learn. We don't have to hold back from blessing our spiritual Sons: we can give sacrificially to see them prosper. As Sons grow up, they will naturally need some separation from their spiritual fathers. Allowing your spiritual Sons to start other Ministries that don't involve you, and might even cost you, will make you a peacemaker and will allow the kingdom of God to expand exponentially. Another benefit of allowing Lot to separate, even allowing him to take the best land, is it serves as an example of God's ability to be a good Father who provides.

Let me throw a quick warning out to Sons. Make sure you learn from your spiritual father how to love God with all your heart. Love God in such a way you are completely sold out to Him, regardless of whether you ever receive a blessing or not. Never take your eyes off the Blesser to chase after blessings.

Abraham is a protector; he does not give up on Lot. He saves him in the physical and intercedes in the supernatural.

Now notice what happens next to Lot.

And Lot lifted up his eyes and saw that the Jordan Valley was well watered everywhere like the garden of the Lord, like the land of Egypt, in the direction of Zoar. (This was before the Lord destroyed Sodom and Gomorrah.) So Lot chose for himself all the Jordan Valley, and Lot journeyed east. Thus they separated from each other (Genesis 13:10-11).

After Lot leaves Abraham to take on what looks like prosperous land, he is actually moving towards Sodom and Gomorrah, two cities filled with more sin than he could ever have imagined. The decision to leave so soon and to trust in his senses will impact

111

the rest of his life. Lot will be kidnapped and have to be rescued. Lot and his family will live in a sinful City and will ultimately have his family torn apart because of their choice to abide in a place where sin is so rampant. So, dear Sons, before you separate from your spiritual fathers, make sure you've heard from your Heavenly Father. Make sure you are called to leave. Leaving too soon might just be an act of Rebellion.

When you take on the role of a spiritual father, you never leave your kids behind, even when they separate from your ministry or your home. So, after Lot leaves, he finds himself in the middle of a war: five rebellious kings of ancient cities are going against four other cities headed up by king Chedorlaormer. Lot finds himself caught up in a war motivated by rebellion which leads to his capture. Abraham learns about this and rescues him, his entourage and everything that was stolen (Genesis 14:1-17).

Abraham raises a bastard and a true son.
Different fathering, different outcomes.

Abraham was a surrogate father to Lot, but He later had two sons of his own. The first was Ishmael, the son with Hagar, birthed out of his own carnal volition to make the promise happen. The second was Isaac, the son of promise with Sarah by a miraculous act of God (Genesis 16:4; 21:203). One was raised as a bastard, the other as a true son.

Pastors, don't take on children that God did not promise to you. How many pastors that carry the promise of a ministry have brought in leaders hastily because they needed the position in the ministry filled, only to realize they have created bastards that have to be released? It was the pastor's promise but not theirs. They are the Ishmaels, positioned for a promise that does not belong to them. No wonder those Ishmaels when they leave, mock, and ridicule us and the legitimate heirs of the promise!

We are all called to have spiritual sons, pastors, business leaders, political leaders, and mechanics. Leaders are all too guilty of the Mr. and Mrs. Right Nows. Be careful that you choose those that God has given you, not those who you have been forced into positioning, for you will damage not only your promise but theirs. When you place temporary people in permanent positions, you are putting them in a place where they are enticed into cursing the promise you were given when their position is removed. They can become bitter from rejection.

We have been guilty of this. Ren in the first few years of ministry had a need to fill the role of a youth pastor. He had been looking for those with the skills and qualifications to fulfill the promise of a healthy fully functioning church with all areas of ministry available. However, by filling those roles too quickly, he took on sons that were not intended to fulfill his promise but someone else's. So when those leaders hit bumps in the road and it became apparent that a separation was needed, it created a huge conflict. The division resulted in wounding both the youth pastor and Ren.

At the same time, some of those leaders got through their season of hurt and now are successfully serving God in their appointed place. Ren still celebrates their success and prays for them because, once you adopt a son, they stay in your heart forever, whether they are prodigals, just estranged, or have grown and matured and are now spiritual fathers with their own flocks.

The church doesn't need hirelings: it needs sons. To paraphrase John 10:12: "Hirelings will run when the wolves show up, so raise up sons who will be shepherds, who will lay down their lives for their sheep." Unfortunately, the hireling conflict always happens at a time when the wolf shows up. It's at that point of conflict that the enemy sees the vulnerability to take that opportunity to pounce on and run off those you were meant to protect.

However, if you produce sons instead, then you will always have leaders ready to fill in the temporary roles needed. Once the Mr. Rights show, sons will gladly move over for them since their current role is not their final identity. Ren took a placement at a church as the music pastor and youth pastor. Filling both roles was tough and Ren had no long term goal of holding on to both. He was a music pastor and the goal was to raise up someone with the heart and calling for the youth, and then release the position. His value did not lie in that position: it lay in being a son of the house.

CHAPTER 8

SIGNS OF A HEALTHY LEADER

The need for spiritual fathers in the church has become so critical because we now have a generation of wayward shepherds. Ultimately, more often than not, the next generation of fathers become like their fathers. Your mentor matters. If our Heavenly Father is your Father, then your likelihood of becoming a good shepherd overwhelmingly tips to your favor. In leadership you have sons, brothers and sheep – never projects. People are not projects. If your foundation is not rooted in love, everything you do to raise up leaders will result in limited fruit. Love is the fertilizer that magnifies the crop field.

What are the characteristics of a good shepherd? How do they treat the sheep they care for? Psalm 23 is probably the most famous of the psalms about the good shepherd. It starts out this way:

The Lord is my shepherd; I shall not want (Psalm 23:1).

God Himself is the Good Shepherd, so His example here will help us better learn how to properly care for and train those that we are raising up.

He makes me lie down in green pastures. He leads me beside still
waters (Psalm 23:2).

Good shepherds don't keep their sheep penned up. Their goal isn't to keep them from ever leaving but, on the contrary, to take them to green pastures. The good shepherd wants them to grow. A good shepherd will bring their sheep to a place of rest by still waters but a bad shepherd will force anxiety and ask those under them to work for results. We have many managers in life but few leaders. Shepherds are called to lead those under them to the best results for the sheep under their charge. Perhaps you have had leaders over you that are just looking for what they can get out of you. Good leaders realize that happy and healthy sheep produce better wool. Fed sheep produce more and better meat.

Even though I walk through the valley of the shadow of death,
I will fear no evil, for you are with me; your rod and your staff,
they comfort me (Psalm 23:4).

A good shepherd uses his staff and rod, or power, to bring comfort to the sheep. The rod is to protect the sheep and the staff is to guide them. Of course, there are two different types of shepherds: those that raise their sheep for the slaughter and those that raise them for the sacrifice. As believers and godly fathers, we are called to be shepherds that raise up sacrificial lambs. Jesus is clear that we are to pick up our cross and follow Him, die daily, and lose our life that we might find it. We are called to be a living sacrifice. In the law of Moses we learn clearly that a lamb the priest sacrificed to God at the altar had to be spotless, without bruise or blemish.

"You shall not sacrifice to the Lord your God an ox or a sheep
in which is a blemish, any defect whatever, for that is an
abomination to the Lord your God..." (Deuteronomy 17:1).

Shepherds that raised up sacrificial lambs know that their lambs have to be without blemish, so beating them was not an option. If you beat your sheep and wound them, they would never be acceptable as a sacrificial lamb. Fathers, we need to stop bruising our sons! The problem lies in our view of the purpose of the sheep. The bad shepherd beats his sheep and leaves them bruised because their only purpose is for the consumption and sustenance of the shepherd or those in the marketplace. They are raised to be devoured by anyone willing to pay up. But the priest, the father, the good shepherd is raising them for the sole purpose of being offered to God: they are set apart for Him.

Fathers, are those you are leading meant to be resources for you? Are they staff or are they God's sons in your eyes? Are they employees of the church or are they sons of the house? Church members or subject to church boards? Sons, do you hire your pastor or is he a father to you? Too many shepherds beat their sheep but too many sheep bite their shepherds in return. If you can fire your pastor, then you do not have a father and you will remain an illegitimate son. Fathers can't be fired. You need to free your pastor to become a father and allow his rod and staff to comfort and guide you.

Sadly, we have seen too many churches run by boards and members, who fire a pastor because they just do not like the direction he is taking them. Since when do the sheep lead the way? Since when is it the sheep's job to lead themselves beside the still waters? When the sheep control the direction, you find chaos. I can't find anywhere in scripture where a pastor is hired. I find nowhere in scripture where sons get to dictate the direction to a father or remove him from power. It was called a coup every time it was tried. David's son Absalom tried to remove him as king; it failed and cost him his life (2 Samuel 15-18).

Fathers are the givers of inheritance and blessing but we have sons that have missed their inheritance because they behave like entitled prodigals. They take without asking and then leave without blessing. Fathers are the bearers of blessing. Jacob received a blessing from his father Isaac. It is amazing how many people leave church regularly and do not understand this spiritual truth, how many people will quietly slip out of church never to be seen or heard from again. They say nothing and tell no one. They pay no mind to the spiritual truth of a father's role of blessing as you depart from their sight. To them, the pastor is not their pastor; he is just the guy running the building where they go to listen until they don't feel like listening anymore. This concept is found nowhere in scripture. In fact, it is quite the opposite. Sheep need a shepherd and, when you find one, you can't have a meeting of the sheep and change the shepherd. Sons need a father; if you don't like what yours says anymore, you don't get to replace him.

I wonder how many people leave church after church because they themselves have been victims of this bastard spirit. How many of them just don't understand that, when they leave a church without a word to the pastor, they rob themselves of the pastor's blessing as they go. If you have just upped and left a church and never said a word to your pastor, then you have contributed to the spread of this bastard spirit in our leaders. Many pastors we meet are leery, and even downright terrified, to get close to "members" because they "know" one fine day they will either leave without a word or will leave with hurtful words. Instead of raising up sons, they have resigned themselves to be spiritual "babysitters."

When those that should be sons treat their fathers as hirelings, they miss the principle of spiritual inheritance. This spirit has perpetuated a vicious cycle. Leaders pour it out on followers; followers pour it out on leaders. We have to stop the cycle!

Leaders, listen up! You need to set the example. We know people will hurt you but you cannot afford to hold the sins of the former members against the new member. We will never believe it is right to condemn an innocent man for the crimes of another. Just because some followers do it, doesn't mean they all will.

Followers, you need to realize that there are leaders who are capable of being good fathers. Let your leaders in and let them have room in your life to mold and shape you into who God has called you to be. Let them stretch you like taffy. If you're called to them, honor them and let them have the opportunity to bless you. Jacob was blessed because of who his father was and because his father had the authority to bless him. I wonder how many leaders have left churches in strife, only to plant new churches full of strife because they did not ask for a blessing. And note that the blessing is positional. Even lackluster fathers have some blessing to give their children.

This is my encouragement and advice to the pastors that have repeated the cycle of being a hireling. They have had boards tell them that they are going a different direction and they have allowed the sheep to control the path. Don't repeat this cycle another time. We know it hurts, but get back up and ask God to bring you sons instead of positions, sheep instead of committees.

Both Terry and Ren are church planters: we started something. Both of us are of the same breed. We don't think we could ever accept a "position." We didn't take a job offer; instead, we birthed a family. Fathers create family; hirelings fill openings. So does that mean you can never fill a vacant leadership role? Of course not, but we need to stop looking at pastor roles as corporate positions instead of covenant relationships. You can step in and be the new stepdad or son of the house. But you are not a hireling.

If you sit in a leadership position and you think the senior pastor of your church works for you, resign your position now. You are walking in direct opposition to the kingdom's established order. You are creating a culture that will treat you the same. You will reap what you sow. Those under you will never be sons and you will find those who need guidance guiding you instead – right into brown pastures and raging waters. It's funny how most churches that suffer this situation are always small and struggling. The sad thing is they truly believe the problem is not being able to find the right pastor. Could it be that God has sent them the right pastor but they are unwilling to follow his lead? If you already know the right direction, then why aren't you there?

What are you missing out on when you do not show your pastor the honor of a spiritual father? When you don't allow him to lead you to calm waters? What would change if you followed him?

Pastors, are you beating your sheep or leading them with comfort? We need both of these –leading and comforting – if we are going to return to the healthy reproductive design God gave us of fathers creating sons, who, in turn, become fathers who create sons. This is the original design to be fruitful and multiply.

There is also a call for the shepherds of the church to raise up sacrificial lambs. The sacrificial lamb is the calling of every Christian. We are called to daily die to ourselves. One amazing thing about dying to yourself – or killing the flesh – is that, when you bury it, it becomes a seed. It is the same principle that Jesus taught of the grain of wheat:

Truly, truly, I say to you, unless a grain of wheat falls into the earth and dies, it remains alone; but if it dies, it bears much fruit (John 12:24).

The seed of sacrificed flesh becomes the harvest of new life. Churches are crying out for revival but are they willing to raise sacrificial lambs? Shepherds, are you more concerned with what you will eat than who you will raise?

CHAPTER 9

RAISING FATHERS AND SONS

So we have identified a serious problem, a gaping hole in our society and, specifically, a huge church problem. We have identified that many ministries struggle to survive more than one generation because of a lack of fathers creating sons. We have no heirs to carry on the Lord's work that those before us created. So what do we do? How do we begin this daunting task of turning the corner? We have to solve this if we want to see this generation's greatest harvest of souls.

Revival is here and we have begun the billion soul harvest. If those who serve in the greatest revival of our lifetime don't raise up those who are called to steward it in the future, then, like every other harvest, it will come and fade, only for the next generation to mourn and long for its return. We will just keep aborting the harvest and then repeating the process over and over. So many others have been held to this groundhog's day of petition. Revival fire breaks out only to be snuffed out by hurt and jealousy, competition and ambition. Could fatherlessness be to blame?

Many great men of God who build the kingdom are treated as assets but never as heirs.

Let's look at what happened in the charismatic renewal revival called the Jesus People Movement. Lonnie Frisbee, the hippie preacher, had helped usher hippies into church – not just a handful but thousands. He helped usher modern music into the church. Yet, while Calvary Chapel had thousands attending, Lonnie Frisbee had to be on food stamps.

I've witnessed many organizations producing popular preachers who drew big crowds and lots of resources. They had anointings on their lives. Yet when those men had a moral failure, the organizations that once supported them turned on them and threw them to the wolves. They used them up, burned them out and then replaced them with the next up-and-coming celebrity pastor. They prostitute your gift while reassuring you that you are loved. Unfortunately, that love is conditional on your anointing performing. Men love you because of your anointing but God anointed you because He loves you.

The bastard spirit seeks to delegitimize your claim of sonship and theirs by nullifying your claim to the kingdom. Don't sell your gifts for acceptance. Don't try to find affirmation from the corrupt kingmakers that will never love you. Even good organizations can fall prey to this condition. Godly leaders who do not fully understand the need to produce sons can see this calamity befall their leadership.

When Ren was much younger, he served at a healthy church he loved dearly. He was used in their music ministry and was often told how valuable his contribution to the house was. His skills and giftings in music and other areas elevated the church. Ren had already been a victim of this bastard spirit and was sensitive and vulnerable to it. He had served there for nearly two years and had a warm relationship with the pastor but truly desired to go deeper. He craved mentoring and family from the leadership and he fought off rejection and insecurity because of past abuses by spiritual mentors.

He still remembers the day his spirit was left bankrupted. He was given a special invitation to have a cookout with the senior pastor. He had only had lunch with the pastor the first time in over two years. Now he was invited to his home. The pastor wanted to honor a few key leaders that were impacting the church. The church had many times bragged before the entire congregation about Ren and his family. Before the day of the invite, something happened and the event was cancelled. But, rather than reschedule the invite, the church changed the format. It became snacks in the church office before and after service with a thoughtful note written to him from the senior staff.

That was the day his heart for the church died. The enemy found his opening and slashed at the scars on his heart. He wanted to be a son but felt like he was just an asset. Yes, he was appreciated but he was not considered worthy to be invited into true intimate relationship. The staff and the church were all very healthy and wonderful people, many of whom he is still connected with today. But he was hurt and unable to shake off the lie of the bastard spirit. This crafty spirit used this one seemingly small moment that was supposed to be a gesture of appreciation as a dagger to the heart of identity.

And so, Ren felt illegitimate. He had access to the pastor's office but not to the home. An heir has access to the home. That day, his value was stolen and he believed he was a servant but not a son. Is that the truth? Probably not, but the bastard spirit works on the scars of the children of God. He blinds the leader to the small events that have huge ramifications. That wonderful pastor probably never even saw that as a possible contributor to Ren's family's ultimate departure. Other things contributed but that was the death blow.

Here's the fruit. The church continued to be a healthy thriving church; Ren did not. He and his family stayed out of church for three years until God would again be given a chance to break off the lies of this spirit, set Ren's family free and restore them back into ministry. A broken heart can be just as damaging to destiny as anger or pride. It can rob you of the ability to navigate your trial and leave you wandering in a desert that you were meant to just simply pass through.

We want to break this bastard spirit before it infects or affects you. Whether you're the leader or the follower, this spirit is looking to devour you either through your actions towards revival or through others' actions against you. Why? Every person we asked wants the same thing, revival! The great revival requires the Great Commission:

"Go therefore and make disciples of all nations, baptizing them in the name of the Father and of the Son and of the Holy Spirit…" (Matthew 28:19)

We are all called to create disciples. It's our job to raise up the next generation and to reproduce what God has grown in us. We need Samuels and the prodigal's dad. We need the image of Jesus that, no matter how many times the disciples missed the boat or missed getting out of the boat, Jesus still told them He would never leave them nor forsake them. It would be great if I told you that the solution to breaking this bastard spirit and the enemy's agenda of fatherlessness, was simply to reassure those we are raising up, that we are not going anywhere and we will stand with them. We will assure them, even when we are bringing correction or having to take disciplinary action, that we love them and will not personally walk away from them.

Unfortunately, however, this is simply not enough. It's a start but it must be built on. The reality is that, if you have been in the church or in leadership for any length of time, chances are you have already encountered this foe of the father's. You have already had this demon of destruction come in and wreck your relationships. So, those that have, are inclined to hesitate to believe the positive reinforcement of those they long to trust and receive life from is more than fluffy words devoid of any weight.

If we want to solve this, then we need to gain back our reputation as spiritual fathers. Like the prophet Samuel, our words should have staying power, none of our words should fall to the ground. They should accomplish the task of carrying the staying power of revival, the staying power of generational blessing, the staying power of churches and ministries to survive to pass the leadership mantle on to the next generation.

How do we go about breaking the bastard spirit? There are several practical things we can do to build our defenses and pull down that stubborn stronghold.

It all Starts with Forgiveness

The first step in breaking this spirit once and for all is forgiveness. It's imperative to let go of the mountain of offenses you have built up against the fathers that failed you. Maybe you need to forgive them; but you, as you read this book, have identified yourself as the failing father. You need to take a leap of forgiveness toward yourself as well. When you do, you'll allow the Lord to catch you in His love. When you forgive, you remove the person that is ultimately being used to hide and protect the bastard spirit from being seen.

126

Forgiveness removes the enemy's armor, not yours.

By keeping you in unforgiveness the enemy is using those that you were meant to love as human shields. They are not a weapon against you; neither are they a shield for the enemy. When you forgive, you move the person aside and get a clear line of sight to bullseye the enemy with the weapons of your warfare. However, when you go after the enemy without first forgiving, you will undoubtedly have collateral damage. You will only wound the person being used as a pawn. The truth is that, if the enemy can distract you, blur your line of sight of him, and get you to engage the person as the problem, then he can and will sneak around. When the fight is done, you will find yourself chained by the enemy. He will put you in bondage.

We meet people all the time that were wounded by real fathers and church fathers. They have authentic and justifiable hurts. What ends up happening in many cases though is the person, full well knowing the damage it has done to them, still repeats this on others they father. They have repeated the cycle over and over, yet they are still angry at the one that did it to them. The key difference between those that break free and those that end up repeating the cycle is the ability to forgive. The enemy doesn't care if you recognize what's going on as long as he is insulated from your ability to do anything about it. Forgiveness is the means to laser target the enemy.

Forgiveness is a choice, period. You must decide to forgive. You must keep no record of wrong. Some of you will need to forgive seventy times seven. It can be a process but I can tell you that, when you forgive, you need to go after the enemy immediately. Otherwise, he will do everything in his power to move the human barricade back in the way and you'll have to forgive all over again. Many times we choose to forgive. But we forget to fight.

We want you to take a second and forgive those that have hurt you. We want you to forgive yourself if you have let others down. It's time to remove the shackles that are preventing you from pressing through to your breakthrough. Forgiveness doesn't necessarily mean entering back into a relationship. It just means that you take your eyes off the person and put them on the enemy. It means you put that person back into God's hands and trust that He, as the real good Father, will do what is right for you and them.

Forgiveness of others is trust in the Lord. Walking in unforgiveness will cost you your peace and joy in the Lord. That is an expensive bill you shouldn't want to pay. Forgiveness breaks the footholds and strongholds this spirit has built. Fathers, forgive yourselves and decide right now that it's time to do better. Forgive sons you've tried to father that broke your heart. Many of you do not father because the pain a natural or spiritual kid caused. Forgive again. Rise up and be the father that our Father has called you to be.

If you need to forgive yourself, then begin to repent for the things you did. Let it out and let it go. As God forgives you, so must you forgive yourself. Repentance is a gift. It is the very manifestation of grace. Because of grace we are offered the opportunity to repent and receive the great do-overs that should not have been available. Repentance is not the pointing out of your sin but rather the pointing to His unending grace. Repentance is the washing in His living water. **Repentance is the tool that repairs the tear between God's divinity and our humanity.** Repent often; forgive often.

Get Them While They're Young

When pastor Ren was just a freshman in high school he was in the choir. Pastor Ren had a burning passion for music that he carried from the age of three. All he ever wanted to do was sing. However, his choir teacher and Ren did not get along. We will call him Mr. Smith to protect the not so innocent. In fact, it was so bad that his choir teacher brazenly pulled Ren up to the front and asked him, "Why are you in my class? You have no talent and no future in music. You are wasting my time and yours." Ren's heart was so wounded, he responded with something like, "Just to make you a living…" Well he wasn't saved yet.

Fast forward two years. Ren is now a junior in high school. He is now saved and starting at a private Christian school. He still has no interest in choir. In steps the female protagonist. Translation: he meets a pretty girl, but she jokes on him; she is a senior, so he can only share electives with her. You may have already guessed it – he finds out she is in the choir. So hurts are trumped by hormones. With reservation, he joins the choir again. His new choir teacher Pastor David Briscoe is also the music pastor of the church there as well as the acting choir director for the school.

At some point that year Pastor David asked Ren to step into his office before service to talk to him. He said he wanted to talk to Ren about his future in music. Oh boy! "Here we go again," he thought! He had heard this speech before and prepared himself for another blow to his identity. "Ren," Pastor David said, 'I want to talk to you about your future in music. I don't know what your plans are but I hope that you pursue music after you leave high school. I'm not talking about just college but I hope you pursue music as a career and as a profession in some form because you are too talented and anointed not to."

Words of life instantly reached in and uprooted the toxic words of death that were planted by the former choir teacher. Those quick few sentences would become a marker in Ren's life. They would shape and shift his view of himself and what was possible for his future. It was a powerful prophetic decree. That word built a strong tower that would defend his destiny. Ren would go on to have an amazing season as a professional musician, playing and working with famous bands and making music with Grammy award winners, touring and recording and, most beloved of all, serving the church as a worship pastor for eighteen years. Through those years of music, the words of pastor David echoed back as an anchor anytime a storm arose.

Since that initial word, many people complimented and spoke life-giving words of encouragement into him and something happens as you get older. The words tend to register more and more as being prophetic. You see, superficial words of flattery can be appreciated but do not have the leverage to shift futures. But words spoken at a crucial time in a young person's life tend to linger and have more power to manifest later in life. Maybe you have a similar story. Words spoken by those that you wanted approval from are still things you ponder and draw either strength or defeat from. While mentoring those that are in their teens and early twenties may require more patience from you, it definitely is easier soil to plow.

I wonder if this is why Jesus' disciples by all accounts were mostly in the late teenage category. Peter was most likely the only disciple over twenty as he and Jesus were the only ones required to pay the temple tax – and one had to be at least twenty years old to do so. Jesus also found them at pivotal points in their life where most of them may have been facing rejection.

The Rabbi model

In the Jewish religious system of Jesus' day, the priest would select his disciples at the age of thirteen to fifteen. It was customary for a child to begin his religious training at the age of five and to continue to age twelve or so. The priest would be on the look out for the best, the brightest and most coveted religious students at thirteen. This is most likely why Jesus was talking with the priest (rabbis) at the temple at the age of twelve. This is why they would have even engaged with Him to begin with (Luke 2:41-50). It was very likely a vetting process to interview a young boy about to come of age for recruitment by the rabbis. By thirteen, as he finished his initial studies, if a boy was intelligent and interested in continuing his religious studies, he would then seek a rabbi to disciple him and would literally follow and pattern his life after the rabbi until age thirty. At that time he was free to take on disciples of his own.

If this pattern holds true with the followers of Jesus, some of them may have joined Jesus as early as age thirteen and would have still been teenagers at the time of His death, resurrection, and ascension. Many of them were already working a trade. Several of the twelve main disciples were fishermen, Matthew was a tax collector, and Simeon was a zealot, which was basically a political activist against Roman occupation. We don't learn about the professions of the other disciples. This is likely due to the fact they were the younger of their contemporary disciples and therefore had not yet been given a trade.

Remember, Jesus did not just have twelve disciples. In Luke 10 we learn that Jesus had appointed seventy disciples. The twelve were the core. These were the ones He drew closer to and mentored at a higher level. So it is likely that most of Jesus' disciples had been passed over for recruitment by other rabbis; many, if not all of those over fifteen would fit this bill. Certainly, Peter, the other fishermen and, definitely, Matthew as a tax collector were more than likely to have already been passed over for recruitment. They would likely have been carrying rejection on them when Jesus found them.

But Jesus spoke life into them and became a true mentor to them. *"Train up a child in the way he should go: and when he is old, he will not depart from it"* (Proverbs 22:6 KJV).

Cover your Father's Iniquity

As Terry and Ren were praying about solutions, one of the stories that popped up was Noah and Ham. We are not going into the full story of whether or not Noah did or did not sin by getting drunk here. Rather, we really want to focus on Noah's sons and how they responded. The three sons came upon a situation in which their father in his own privacy had passed out, drunk and naked. This was seriously awkward for any son. At least it wasn't Mom because then it goes from awkward, to scarred for life. Shem and Japheth, upon hearing from Ham the state he found their father in, decided to cover their father with their coat. They even went so far as to walk the coat backwards so as not to even see his nakedness (Genesis 9:21-23).

My question would be this. What would be your response to your spiritual fathers, including the ones who have operated under the bastard spirit? How would you respond to their weaknesses? Would you act like Ham and take delight in that moment? Would you revel in the fact you caught your father in nakedness, in drunkenness, and in iniquity? Or would you take the righteous holy choice and let go of the devoted things belonging to the Lord? One of the devoted things we have to let go of is judgment of the Lord's anointed. It is not yours to hold on to, for judgment belongs to the Lord.

We also have an opportunity to walk out the Old Testament and the Commandments. The Commandments say, "Honor your mother and father and it will go well with you and you'll live long in the land and prosper (That's a Spock from Star Trek blessing that is being offered to all of us! Live Long and Prosper!!). In order to receive the blessing, you must honor your father! So here's the decision you get to make. Will you revel in the iniquity? Will you call it out all the time? Will you point at every person you get the opportunity to, like Ham did? You have another choice. Will you do like Shem and Japheth and turn your back to the iniquity, take the covering that Christ covers you with, rest it on your shoulders and walk backwards to cover the iniquities of your father?

We have to understand that, even when Saul was a bad father, murderous and competing with his son, he still held an anointing on him that God would not revoke. If we mess with God's anointed, we mess with God Himself. When we war against God's anointed, we war against God. Don't believe me?

Look at what happened when David found out who cut off the head of Saul, his spiritual father. This was the same Saul who pursued him into the wilderness, who threatened to kill him, who tried to destroy him, who tried to rob him of his legacy, who showed no mercy or love towards him. Look at David's response to the one who cut off Saul's head. David, grieving for Saul, had the man executed. I'm sure the soldier who took Saul's life thought he would find favor with David because at the time David was fighting on the enemy's side. Yet, when he heard that this soldier had killed Saul, David without hesitation ended the soldier's life (2 Samuel:1-15). I don't know about you, but my intention is never to cut off the heads of Sauls in our generation.

It was Saul's own insecurities that robbed him of the ability to see that he had a son that, had he just treated as an heir instead of an enemy, would have loyally defended him and his kingdom. But Saul, like Ham, could not see the damage he was doing in their lack of covering. While a father is meant to cover their son. there are times that sons can cover their fathers, too. Noah had two good sons as cover for him but Saul was an insecure father. An insecure father cannot receive covering from your son, just as a rebellious son cannot cover his father with anything but condemnation. Protect your father's identity. Speak life over him to everyone and praise him at every chance possible.

Cultivate Intimacy in Relationship

The story of Eli we shared holds a great key to being raised into a spiritual father. In 1 Samuel 3 we read about Samuel's first encounter with the voice of God. At first, when Samuel hears God's voice, he is confused and thinks it is the voice of Eli because Samuel is most intimate with Eli and mistakes God's voice for his. He gets up and goes to find Eli. Now it's interesting that Samuel needs to find Eli. Why? Was Eli not where he was supposed to be? No, he was in the priests' sleeping quarters. It was Samuel that is the one in an odd place. It says Samuel was sleeping in the tabernacle where the ark of the covenant was held, right outside the Holy of Holies. He is as close to the manifest presence as he can get.

Our ability to draw close to His presence will unlock encounters with His glory. If the tent is where He dwells, then that's where we need to seek Him. If we are near Him, we can hear Him. Spending time in conversation and having a lifestyle of being in communication with Him daily is a key to intimacy. Our intimacy with God will determine our ability to hear Him.

Again, Samuel was prepared for an encounter. In order to enter the tabernacle you had to be clean. You had to be clothed in priestly garments. Samuel shows us that a key to intimacy with Father God is that we stay in a state of living holy. Living holy allows us to draw as close as possible to His presence. The word says that Christ clothes us in righteousness. What an interesting paradox that it is Jesus Himself that prepares us for His intimate presence. We don't make ourselves righteous. He makes us righteous; we simply walk in that righteousness.

Notice it's not when Samuel is laboring to fulfill his priestly duties that God speaks to him. God speaks to Samuel when he is in a quiet restful state.

"Be still, and know that I am God. I will be exalted among the nations, I will be exalted in the earth!" (Psalm 46:10)

You need to position yourself to hear God, not labor for it. It is when we quiet ourselves and listen for Him that we best can encounter Him. If all you ever do in prayer is present Him with your request or worship, but never learn to rest in His presence, it can be easy to miss the still small voice of God when it comes. You need to learn in those quiet moments that His voice can appear to be your own. When there is too much background noise, it becomes strenuous to tell if the person talking is Ren or one of his three sons. They are sixteen, eighteen and twenty years old and sound so much like Ren. It's not till the room quiets that you can finally make a distinction between their voices. The quieter you are, the easier it will be to distinguish between God's voice, man's voice or the voice of the enemy. Get close to Jesus; get your eyes on Him, then get quiet and get still. Wait and listen to every thought that enters and write it down. When you read it back, you may find that God has been speaking to you.

Labor in Rest

Finally, we need to learn to *labor in rest*. No, that's not an oxymoron. We need to stay in that state of rest. Often, out of a fear of being valueless we try to earn value by what we do and accomplish. I don't work *for* acceptance, I work *from* acceptance. I don't work *for* love, I work *from* love. We can learn to rest in Him and let Him do the heavy lifting. The Good Shepherd doesn't just lead you to a place of rest but to a state of rest. He wants to equip you *in the power* of rest. You can always tell someone who even prays out of rest.

One of the best impartations that Ren received was from Dr. Alan Hawkins. Ren had never seen someone minister in rest the way he did. His eyes were opened when he prayed over people. In his eyes Ren saw both peace and power. He would spend as much time as needed on each individual with no concern for the time it would take to make it through the waiting line. He was restful and joyful. Something was imparted over Ren by Dr. Alan, and Ren learned to operate in rest. Ministering for fourteen to sixteen hours, day after day, on crusades in Africa, he never needed rest. Then the final day would come and, after the final session, the demand for a break would wash over his body.

God can sustain you when you just rest in Him. Ren never strives in prayer. Many times when we pray, it's as though we believe we need to pray hard enough, squint our eyes, raise our voices until God is pleased with our strenuous exhausted efforts and will finally give in to our plea. He is a good Father; it's the bastard spirit that makes us think we need to keep begging our Heavenly Father or He will ignore our requests.

Once, Ren had a vision when he was speaking to the Lord about what co-laboring looked like. The Lord showed Ren an aerial view of Himself lying on the ground with wheat thrown about the ground under Him. And He was laughing and talking. As the image began to pull back up into the sky, the view widened and Ren could see a circle of already threshed wheat all around Him. The image pulled back even further and Ren now could see Jesus standing at the edge of the circle where the wheat was still waiting to be harvested. Jesus was holding the harvesting sickle and was swinging it steadily to bring in the harvest. He was working, laughing and conversing with Ren the whole time. The Lord spoke to Ren and said, "You need to learn to co-labor with Me this way. I reap the harvest; you just spend time with Me as I do."

It is the intimate time we spend with Him that He is looking for. He is the one that draws men (wheat) unto Him. He is just looking for our intimate time. This doesn't mean we are idle –

no, not at all. But it does mean it is not "work" to work for the Lord: it is joy and it is peace. When Ren stops at a restaurant to pray for someone or prophesy over them, it is not out of a work mentality. It is out of the same childlike spirit that would lie in the wheat field just to talk to Dad but would have no trouble getting up to play if a child showed up suddenly.

In that same spirit, I'm not working to share the gospel or show the power of heaven. I'm playing with a sibling. Sharing our faith, living out loud and leaning into our call to go and make disciples is how the Father is releasing us to play. We need to leave the striving for the enemy – let him wear himself out trying to keep up with how much we harvest in play. At some point we have to catch the revelation that, at the very core of our relationship with God, He is not looking for a ditch digger, He is looking for a son. Rest: God does not want you to be His CEO but His son. Rest: our intimacy secures our identity.

Rest is a powerful tool and weapon to see God's power on the earth. It is the unstoppable flash of flood waters that washes over the parched land of famine and dry bones of your soul to restore, replenish and refresh that which God had redeemed and released in you. Stop working *for* intimacy with God and work *from* intimacy with God. Fathers, give away your intimacy easily. Our Heavenly Father does this for you and you should do it for those around you as well. Fathers, your sons need your intimacy just as you need it from Father God. When your spiritual sons do not feel like they have to labor for your love, then you are protecting them from failure and stumbling on their journey.

From experience, I can tell you when most people are the most susceptible to sin. It's when the crack in their armor becomes an open door that leads to the darkness pouncing on our souls and this often happens when we are tired. Physical or emotional tiredness is an enemy to righteousness and obedience. Most people can stick to their diets all day but, man, when the sun sets, so does our will power. You find the 10.00 pm binging becomes like the call of a siren, beckoning you, "Come eat me!" It's late at night that most people fall into porn or even engage in adultery.

When our emotions are surrendered to Jesus and in line with His word, they are a powerful ally. But when we are tired, our emotions can drag us off course if we aren't careful. Taking care of ourselves by resting and eating right to give your body the fuel it needs to properly heal in rest is crucial in the war for your spiritual growth. If you have been married for any length of time, then you should already know that a tired spouse is not an intimate spouse. An unhealthy spouse is not an intimate spouse. Why would it be any different with our intimacy with God? These are signs of the flesh warring against our spirit.

If the enemy can't stop you, then he'll wind you up and watch you run. A sprinter always runs faster than a marathon runner but a marathon runner is still in the race when the sprinter can't take another step. Our walk is over a lifetime, so stop letting the enemy convince you that you're being left behind if you don't prove you can run the fastest. Rest, go at the pace God has called you to. Maybe now you can fully catch the power of this scriptures.

> *Even youths shall faint and be weary, and young men shall fall exhausted; but they who **wait for** the Lord shall renew their strength; they shall mount up with wings like eagles; they shall run and not be weary; they shall walk and not faint* (Isaiah 40:30-31, emphasis added).

The word "wait" here is the Hebrew verb, *qavah*, which is in a tense that implies "lie in wait," or "linger" for. Wow! It's just like the vision the Lord showed Ren earlier. To lie in rest is to work with the Lord and wait on Him to show up and meet you with His strength. You can run and not grow weary when you *run in rest*. What a deep and marvelous mystery! The original meaning of that word *qavah* most likely means "bound together by twisting," like strands coiling into a rope. So we don't just lie in wait but we are twisted together, corded together. God does the heavy lifting; He is the rope, we just rest in Him as one of the strands. That's the great thing about rope strands: no one strand does all the work. In fact, we are just one strand but He's the bunch. Let Him pull you through – you just rest in Him.

The account of Martha and Mary should drive this point home. One labored in the kitchen for Jesus and the other sat at His feet. When Martha had asked Jesus to get on to Mary, Jesus let us know that Mary was right where she should be. When He's in the room, stop and rest at His feet. This is the unlocked mystery that Jesus practiced. He said that He only did what He saw the Father do. He followed Dad around everywhere. Where Father God went, so did Jesus, right at His feet. Learn to be in the room. It's a room of rest. Let Him pour out the miracle, and follow Him and your walking will never lead to fainting. Maybe that's why Jesus was so insistent on letting the little ones come to Him. The sermons we preach, the people we pray for, the time we spend in prayer and study should all be in the mode of just sitting at His feet in rest.

CHAPTER 10

WHO'S LEADING?

While we have a void of spiritual fathers in the world, one of the contributions to the bastard spirit is those who have the heart for it but do not have the time or focus for it. Your first statement to a potential spiritual father should be, "Do not take me on as a son, if you don't have time to raise me." When a mentor enters your life and you are prayerfully considering the call to come under their leadership, this should be your first question.

Too many wonderful, well meaning and gifted leaders have desired to raise up other leaders but find they just don't have the time to devote to their stewarding. This could be either because they just have too many other commitments or they have taken on too many spiritual sons. The old phrase goes, a child left to themselves will self-destruct. This works in the spirit, too. When a leader takes on too many to raise, it creates the empty space for the bastard spirit to begin to work on the one being raised up.

You don't have to be a son or a father to someone to be in a relationship, even a covenant relationship. Terry and Ren, for example, are writing this book together in covenant partnership. Ren is not Terry's daddy even though he is technically two years older and tries to pull seniority. No, we are brothers and we are sharpening each other. What we have found in this process of working together, bouncing our ideas back and forth, how much deeper and revelatory our understanding of the father role is. While we are playfully competing in this writing blitz – and it is actually making the book come to life in ways we did not anticipate – a father could help minimize the impact of negative competition in leadership structures.

Fathers are crucial because brothers always seem to compete. Those on an equal level often find competition creeping in, an associate pastor competing with the youth pastor, the marketing manager competing with the sales manager, students competing with one another for top grades. Joseph was clearly no stranger to that reality with his brothers.

So how are the two of us handling all that when we have had no true spiritual father? You may be saying to yourself that you don't yet have a spiritual father either. This truth does not leave us hopeless or helpless. God is amazing at raising sons. While man may be limited on time or focus, Father God is not limited by either. He has made it very clear to both of us that, while He has not given us spiritual fathers as yet, until that day, He Himself will be our Father and raise us up as godly men. If you do not yet have a spiritual mentor, don't let that get you feeling you have to make it on your own. I promise, when the time comes, God will bring you one.

Let Him bring you that promise when it's ripe, lest you end up being a self-created Ishmael and adding to the bastard mindset that isn't meant for you. Don't try to claim a father that will never give you his name. No name, no inheritance. When you try to take on a father that is not legitimately supposed to be yours, you actually create self-inflicted wounds of rejection, bitterness and unforgiveness. And, like Ishmael, it will lead you to mocking the Father's legitimate children who have the promise of blessing on them.

We all need to learn that there are different positions in covenant relationships. There are sons, fathers, brothers, and sheep. Each serves a crucial role in our lives and we need each one. Brothers can sharpen each other at the same time. A leader is not a leader without a follower, so shepherds need sheep. You can't be a good leader until you have truly learned to follow, so sheep need shepherds. Some of our relationships are sheep relationships, some are brother relationships and some are mentoring relationships, and we need all three.

Don't Let Failure Keep You from Fathering.

For many years, Ren has had a great man of God in his life that has been a friend, a mentor, a correcting rod and spiritual family to him. Ren held him in high esteem and looked to him as a father figure. He often told him, "You are like a father to me." Yet this man would always brush off that statement and tell Ren that they were brothers sharpening each other. This felt like yet another rejection, another man who did not see enough value in Ren to be a father to him. Their relationship continued and after years it truly grew into an iron sharpening iron relationship as brothers.

As Ren was discussing this book with his dear friend, his friend made a startling omission. He told Ren that the only reason he did not accept the identity of being a spiritual father those many years ago was, not because of any deficit in Ren or the way he felt about Ren, but rather his own insecurity. He felt like he would fail as a spiritual father. If he took on that role, he would not have the wisdom to father Ren correctly. Holding back tears, he apologized to Ren. The truth is Ren would have taken him imperfect just the

143

way he was. You see, this man had a heart after God and a heart for Ren. That was enough for Ren.

Do not hold back from those that you clearly influence and who clearly want your guidance. You may not be fully equipped to father just yet, but even in the natural world isn't that always the case?

CHOOSE WISELY

If you want to break this bastard spirit, both spiritual fathers and those they father have to realize that you are not called to everyone. You cannot simply gather anyone and everyone to raise you. We meet people all the time whose entire identity is wrapped up in one question, "Why won't anyone love me and claim me?" As sons, they try to make anyone older a father or, as fathers, they try to get everyone to become their sons. When Ren counsels young people through breakups, he hears this line all the time. "I'm never going to find anyone to love. Every relationship I have falls apart." Ren's reply is always the same. "Every relationship you have will fail, until the last one. You're only going to have one successful relationship. If the relationship is not God's choice for you, then it's better that if fails quicker."

You can have more than one spiritual parent and son but you can't have more than you can be intimate with. Jesus had seventy disciples that He sent out. Out of the seventy, twelve were in the inner circle, and only three were in a deep intimate relationship with Him. If that was the most Jesus fathered, then we should understand that we only need a handful of these relationships at a time in order to properly steward them. When we take on more sons than we can handle, we can't help but unintentionally ignore or neglect them, which opens the door wide open for the bastard spirit to wreak mayhem in your lives.

If you have done this, you need to reach out to those you father, and repent. Make sure that they know it's your failure and not an indictment of their lovability. Create a healthy cycle. Raise them up and, as they mature, they will need you less and less. Then, when their lack of need results in them raising their own spiritual families, you can take on more sons.

Sons, if you want to find a spiritual dad, don't go around with the attitude that, when someone recognizes the calling you carry, then you'll get busy laboring. Do not let fathers find you idle. You will attract father figures to you when they find you in the field already. Elisha received the first mantle when Elijah found him plowing. He received the second one while he was pursuing Elijah to receive a double anointing (1 Kings 19:19; 2 Kings 2:9).

If you want God to use you for mighty things, then get under a father and take care of his sheep.

When we look for someone to father, it is not amongst fan stands. We don't look amongst those cheering for Jesus but those on the playing field that need a coach. God made David the shepherd a king. God made Moses the shepherd the deliverer. When you are adopted by a father, stay in that sonship positioning, and heed wise counsel with respect and honor. When a disagreement arises, do not seek out another father, but seek the Lord. Abhor self-promotion. As long as you are properly aligned, your spine will be straight, your nervous energy will flow in peace, and you will be covered. In this positioning, the enemy must go through your father to get to you! When you do that, you will find very quickly that God will use you and fathers will see you. Help your leader with the people he is charged with stewarding. Just keep caring for a father's sheep.

To break this bastard spirit, we need to know thy enemy. We may think these bad dads are the enemy, but they're not. Our afflicted fathers are not the enemy. The enemy is the afflicting spirit. Our fathers are not the bastards, for this is a full out assault on the hearts of our leaders. We need to have a correcting spirit, not a critical spirit, for those that are caught as prisoners of war in this conflict. We have to set the captives free, not finish them off.

We spoke with Dr. Mike Hutchings from Global Awakening. Dr. Mike runs Randy Clark's school and is widely known for helping people break trauma off their lives. We asked him how that large organization runs and whether they have employees or sons. His response was that he very purposefully fills the role of a spiritual father of the school. The first and second year students each have a pastor over them. Dr Mike is the father to those pastors and those pastors, in turn, father the interns out of the school and the interns help father many of the students. They are not employees but sons of the house.

There is a strong culture of honor. We have seen the fruit out of the house. The sons they produce are anointed, honoring, powerful, humble and kind. Even when the organization grew too big for Dr Mike to father everyone, they made sure they had a system in place to keep the line of legacy intact. Their spiritual inheritance is ensured and they freely give sons position, honor and impartation. They are engaged in their staff's lives. While many organizations have an, "if you fail policy," Global seems to have a "keep you from failing policy."

All too often we see reactionary ministries at many churches that help people cope after the fact. I see lots of churches with divorce recovery ministries to help people cope with divorce but I see very few marriage strengthening ministries. If the church would take on the call to father our young married couples sooner, maybe we could limit how many broken relationships are breaking our people. Sadly, much of the church is set up that way.

A natural father is there from day one of a child's life. He teaches him how to ride a bike, not just pick him up when he falls down. Our pastors can't walk with everyone all the time. That means we all need to be spiritual parents. Spiritual parents can save them from falling so many times in the first place.

How to lose a dad in ten days?
The easiest way is to complain that he is not doing enough for you. Complain he is not promoting and positioning you fast enough. Fathers and sons need to steward patience. Impatience is a window the bastard spirit uses to gain a clear line of sight to attack you through. Learn to protect people's positioning by categorizing them correctly. Not everyone is meant to be your son. Not properly understanding someone's relationship with you can be harmful to both your and their mental, emotional and spiritual health.

Ultimately, this is a spirit that produces a destructive mindset. It's not a person, so we must pursue a spiritual solution. We need to declare war on this demonic force and pray to break this spirit off and shut all the openings through which this thief is gaining access to steal from us.

This may be a book you need to reread many times to catch the full revelations but the goal is for our churches to begin to become spiritual fathers that begin to raise up godly sons and daughters who, in turn, raise up their own. We want to be a healthy organism that reproduces healthy offspring. When we do, I believe we will begin to unlock revival and more of God's presence as we fulfill the great commission of making disciples. Don't just make converts. Don't just make students. Don't just make servants. Make sons. Your role may be to educate some. Sometimes you are just there to win them to Jesus. Sometimes you just serve with them as brothers and sisters in Christ but, if you have not collected some spiritual kids along the way, it may be time to step up and make some spiritual adoptions.

Let's raise up the next godly generation! Let's raise up the next holy nation, one that will steward God's presence in all the earth. It's time to take back the nations!

> I will proclaim the Lord's decree: He said to me, "You are my son; today I have become your father. Ask me, and I will make the nations your inheritance, the ends of the earth your possession" (Psalm 2:7-8 NIV).

What Now?
We would love to finish this book with a compact "Ten Ways to be a Spiritual Father" and leave you with a list of things you can just simply duplicate and see spiritual sons and daughters raised. Unfortunately, it just won't work that way. The danger in doing that is you will turn relationship and intimacy into a method and a factory. You cannot have a step-by-step manual for sons, for it would not make them sons but employees. Employees have manuals and sons have loving families. We can't tell you how much time to spend with them every week because each will be different at each level. We can't tell you how strong your corrections should be or how much praise you have to heap on them.

So we will avoid the hard-and-fast methods and just lay out some models that can be great starting points for you.

1. Invest your resource of time in your spiritual children. The same way that biological children need a father's time, so do your spiritual children. Your time together needs to be

intentional. It should be personal; it should train, equip and grow the relationship. It needs to also be fun. Don't forget to enjoy the time you spend together.

2. Do not take on a son that cannot be corrected. Correction needs to be clearly defined as a part of the process of showing love.

3. As sons grow, you need to give them your name. You need to release them to be able to take on responsibility, and use your influence until they can build their own.

4. Teach them the word of God. Lead them by example. Pray over them and also pray with them. As they mature, have them pray over you. Raise spiritual children up in the way they should go and they will not depart from it.

5. Speak life! It is essential that every chance you get, don't just dish out compliments of the super job and atta boys they are but speak words of destiny over them. You must prophesy purposefully over them regularly.

6. Position them with authority. As they mature to handle it, it is crucial you increase their role. Hand off tasks and leadership assignments to them as you continue to equip them. Let them begin to rise up into their anointing and duplicate your own authority. Let them stand on your shoulders and raise them higher than yourself.

These are few reminders of practical ways you can begin to raise your spiritual children. This book is chock full of nuggets of wisdom and we hope that these revelations have leaped off the pages at you. Our advice is simple. Read it again. As you read it again, take note of all the actions you can take to raise up the next generation of leaders, sons, daughters, businessmen, fathers and mothers.

We've buried this treasure all throughout the book as we wrapped our own experiences around the principles laid out. Why not just put them in one little section nice and neat? Because you just wouldn't catch all the revelation in a step-by-step formula. This is about growing a heart for spiritual kids. You cannot make a loving relationship a formula. So the truth needs to grab your heart one revelation at a time.

Our parting word is to charge fathers to go change the world and create generations of world changers behind you. Let this go from two fathers to all the fathers reading this book. We bless you in raising your sons. We declare that your anointing will be poured out into a thousand generations and the world will be changed by you releasing what you carry from the Father of us all.

NOTES

....

....

....

....

....

....

....

....

....

....

....

....

....

....

....

....

....

AUTHOR BIOS

Pastor Terry Cuthbertson is the senior pastor of Hope City Church in Arcadia, Oklahoma, a suburb of Oklahoma City. He is an ardent follower of Jesus, a church planter, revivalist, speaker, health coach and kingdom entrepreneur who walks in a healing and prophetic anointing. Terry is known for his governmental entrepreneur mantle that he releases over the community and business leaders to see increase and favor.

In 2017 Pastor Terry planted a church and received a life-shifting impartation from Pastor Rod Parsley, which began an outpouring of Holy Spirit power through his ministry.

Pastor Terry is the founder of Prayerloops.com and can now add author to his bio. He has been featured on popular online broadcasts frequently as well as satellite TV stations: Praise TV, Eternal Fire TV, King TV, and more.

Pastor Terry is a husband and father, and an unusually young grandfather. His wife Nina and his three children, Alyssa, Ayla, Ashton and grandson Beckett are his greatest blessing.

Follow him on his social media pages:
Facebook: @tcuthbertson
Instagram: @pastortokc
Parler: @Tcuthbertson
YouTube: Hope City Church OK
www.hopecityokc.church

Pastor Ren Schuffman is the senior pastor of Freedom Fellowship Church in Mustang Oklahoma, a suburb of Oklahoma city. He flows in a strong healing and prophetic anointing and is known for his gift of imparting a double gifting over those for whom he prays. As a church planter, musician, international speaker and revivalist, Pastor Ren and the ministry have been featured on God TV, Charisma Podcasts, Destiny Image Podcasts, Morningstar, satellite TV, and more.

Pastor Ren was called into the ministry as a teenager while attending Southwestern Christian University, and he served in every position in the church following. As a music pastor over a long period, he spent several years on tour in a Christian Rock band called StoneWater until the Lord called him to plant a church in 2016.

In 2018 Pastor Ren was at Global Awakening and was prayed over by many in that house, including Randy Clark. In was here that Pastor Ren received a life-shifting impartation that launched him into a season of the outpouring of healings, signs and miracles.

Pastor Ren is married to Rachael and is a father of three boys, Isaiah, Eli and Caleb. Rachael Schuffman serves Freedom Fellowship as a pastor and heads the emotional healing ministries.

Pastor Ren can be seen around the world on satellite television. He is featured in Charisma Magazine and hosts a podcast on their network. He also hosts the Power Hour of Prayer. This live internet broadcast reaches around the world. Pastor Ren has anointed pastors from across the globe as guests that release the supernatural over those watching with healing and prophecy happening nightly.

You can watch them live every weeknight @ 8.00 pm Central time at www.youtube.com/freedomfellowship

Follow him on his social media pages:
Facebook: @pastorrenofficial
Instagram: renschuffman
Twitter: renschuffman
Parler: @renschuffman
Youtube: freedomfellowship
www.ffc.church